THE HARD AND THE HOLY

WHAT THE BOOK OF LEVITICUS MEANS FOR TODAY

Written by Kayla Ferris

All Scripture quotations are English StandardVersion (ESV) unless otherwise noted.

We must exchange whispers with God before shouts with the world.

LYSA TERKEURST

PAIR YOUR STUDY GUIDE WITH THE FIRST 5 MOBILE APP!

This study guide is designed to accompany your study of Scripture in the First 5 mobile app. You can use it as a standalone study, or as an accompanying guide to the daily content within First 5.

First 5 is a free mobile app developed by Proverbs 31 Ministries to transform your daily time with God.

Go to the app store on your smartphone, download the First 5 app and create a free account!

WWW.FIRST5.ORG

WELCOME TO LEVITICUS

What words come to mind when you think about the book of Leviticus? I recently presented this question online and could relate to the answers. There were many who said "laws" or "rules." One person put it as "unattainable expectations." Some said "boring," "scary," "sorrow" or one that made me chuckle, just "don't." And then there was one person's response that echoed my thoughts exactly as I wrapped up writing this guide. She called Leviticus "more interesting than I thought."

Oh, friends, I cannot explain how excited I am for you to walk through this study with me. Leviticus is a fascinating book — one that has grown my faith and love for God like I never expected. Can it be hard? Absolutely. There are hard sections, and we are not going to shy away from the hard parts. We are going to walk through them, together, with biblical context and scholarly help along the way. Something precious happens when we press into the hard: We also find the holy. There is a sense of awe and respect and even gratitude and joy that comes from seeing the holiness of God on display. Leviticus is both hard and holy, and that combination is so, so good.

But even more than showing you the hard and holy, I pray this study will show you exactly what those hard and holy parts of Leviticus can mean for you today. The key to this is going to be pulling back the curtain from these laws. Laws show us the values of the law-giver. Our goal is to use Leviticus to show us the heart of God. And when we find the heart behind the law, we will understand how His heart still applies to us today. The God we serve is *"the same yesterday and today and forever"* (Hebrews 13:8). His heart for us never changes! Therefore, we have so much to learn about God from this dive into Levitical law.

So go ahead. Write down those words that come to mind when you think of Leviticus. It's OK to be honest. But here's the catch: I challenge you to come back here in eight weeks, when this study is done, and see how the Spirit transforms those words into more than you could ever imagine!

Hang on tight, friends. We are diving straight into the deep end, pushing past the surface, pressing through the hard, until we find the holy awaiting us. And the view down there, with God's heart on display, will change our lives if we let it. Welcome to the book of Leviticus.

Interesting Fact About Leviticus:

In the ESV translation of Leviticus, the word "holy" (*qā·ḏôš* in Hebrew) is used an astonishing **92 times** across 78 verses!

What word(s) come to mind when you think about the book of Leviticus?

WHAT YOU MIGHT DISCOVER FROM STUDYING LEVITICUS

A BETTER UNDERSTANDING OF HOLINESS

Holiness can feel daunting or even scary. We know that God is holy, but do we really grasp what that means? And how can we even begin to walk toward holiness? Studying Leviticus has helped me see "holiness" as a beautiful word. The holiness of God is what I long for, and it is what will make our time in heaven so wonderful and perfect. I'm so thankful to worship a God who can do no wrong!

A DEEPER RESPECT FOR GOD

I have been reminded throughout Leviticus that God is God, and I am not. He is in charge. He is all-powerful and all-knowing, and He is the Creator. As such, He has the authority and right to lay out rules for His creation. Because of His holiness (as we just talked about), I know that His ways are always right and good. Therefore, I can trust Him, even when obedience feels hard. I've also come to learn that it is OK that some parts feel hard. As Pastor Tim Keller once said, "If your god never disagrees with you, you might just be worshiping an idealized version of yourself." [2]

A RICHER LOVE FOR JESUS

This is the one that really blows me away. What could Old Testament law have to do with Jesus? Everything. All of it points to Him. The sacrifices, the feasts, the laws and rules — all of it. I not only have a better understanding of what Jesus' life and sacrifice mean, but I have a greater appreciation and love for what He did. He is my sacrifice. He takes away my sin. He covers me — sinful, fumbling, fallen me — in His holiness. Oh, what a Savior!

Get ready, friends. Leviticus just might surprise you by all that is waiting to be discovered!

WHO WROTE LEVITICUS?

In order to properly discuss who wrote the book of Leviticus, we have to broaden our question to "Who wrote the Pentateuch?" The Pentateuch, sometimes referred to as the Torah, includes the first five books of the Hebrew Bible. We know those five books as Genesis, Exodus, Leviticus, Numbers and Deuteronomy.

These books flow, one to another, and even if they were penned by others, it is undisputed that much of the divine revelation was expressed to God's people through a man named Moses. You might be familiar with Moses as the man who brought down God's Ten Commandments from Mount Sinai. Having grown up in an Egyptian palace, Moses would have been well educated.

We are told in Deuteronomy 31:9 that *"Moses wrote this law and gave it to the priests."* Verse 24 says that Moses *"finished writing the words of this law in a book to the very end."* While we cannot be sure this included the book of Leviticus, it would certainly fit within the context. Also, within the book of Leviticus, we find many times the phrase *"The LORD spoke to Moses ..."* which, again, indicates little doubt that Moses had a big influence on this book.

Assuming Moses was the author (as most scholars do), the book of Leviticus was likely written around 1500 B.C. It flows right off of the book of Exodus, where the last chapters were dedicated to describing the tabernacle-building process and establishing the priesthood. It makes sense that the next step would be to outline exactly what was to take place within this tabernacle and to provide a description of the duties the priests were to perform.

In Hebrew, the book we are studying is called *wayyiqra'*, which means, "and he called." These are the first words of the book. However, when the Pentateuch was translated into Greek (we call this the Septuagint), this book was then referred to by a Greek word, *leyitikon*, which literally translates to "things concerning Levites." From this, translators later transformed it into the English word "Leviticus."

And so it is that "God called" a man named Moses to give him the rules and regulations of "things concerning Levites." However, it was not just the Levites (Israelite priests) who benefitted from Leviticus. It was not even just the ancient nation of Israel, or the Jewish people. Leviticus has much to teach us, as Christians today, about God's heart and plan for all of humanity.

Interesting Fact About Leviticus:

Traditionally, Leviticus was the first book taught to Jewish children.

LEVITICUS IN CONTEXT

If I were to come up to you and yell "MOVE!" you might think I was an incredibly rude person or it might make you angry. However, if you were standing in the street and a car was heading right toward you when I yelled, it could save your life, and you might call me a hero. The context of the action is everything.

Context is going to be so critical when studying the book of Leviticus. But what exactly is context? The Cambridge dictionary defines it as "the situation within which something exists or happens, and that can help explain it." [1] In other words, we cannot fully understand Leviticus unless we pay attention to what surrounds it, such as the time period it was set in, the people it was directed toward and the purpose it was meant to accomplish.

Leviticus was written around 1500 B.C. Before this time, there was no "nation of Israel." A single family (Israel and his 12 sons) had entered Egypt. Eventually this family line became slaves. When they left Egypt, scholars believe Israel's descendants had grown to a group of as many as 2 million people. As they headed out into the wilderness, fresh out of slavery, to start their own nation, they needed clear guidelines on how to go forward. How were they to govern themselves?

Leviticus was also written to a specific group of people. This tribe was to be God's chosen people for a special purpose. They were meant to bless the entire world! (Genesis 12:1-3) They had the enormous responsibility of reflecting the holy God to all nations. To do so, God wanted them to set themselves apart from others. In Exodus 19:6a, God called them *"a kingdom of priests."* The role of a priest is to help others in their relationship to God. This was to be the role of Israel.

As we read Leviticus, keep in mind the new nation that was being born in this dark and violent time. They had a very specific job to fulfill. Remember this to put the proper perspective on the laws and rituals that may seem foreign to us today. One of the reasons some people give for not studying Leviticus is that it is hard to understand, and part of that is because we are unfamiliar with the culture and times. One of the great parts of this study is that we are going to fill in some of that context so that we can understand the rich meaning within the laws of Leviticus. As we take a step back in time, we will see just how much it has to teach us today.

THE THREE CATEGORIES OF LAW

Within Leviticus, we will find three different categories of law. Knowing these will help us put the different laws into perspective to understand how they apply to us today.

CEREMONIAL (OR RITUAL) LAW

Ceremonial laws had to do with animal and grain sacrifices. These were laws that had to do with staying "clean" (like what foods you could or could not eat, when and what to wash, etc.) as well as "holy days" such as Sabbath and Day of Atonement.

Ceremonial laws became obsolete with the sacrifice of Jesus. He became the only sacrifice needed. His blood washes us and makes us clean before God. He is Lord of the Sabbath and our Day of Atonement. Many of the ceremonial laws show us a beautiful foreshadowing of Christ.

CIVIL LAW

These are laws and punishments that were set up to govern the society of ancient Israel. This was their judicial system. These were laws meant specifically for this nation in this time period. And while these laws are no longer applicable to society today, we can still look to the heart underneath the law to show us the message and values of God, which are never changing.

MORAL LAW

Also within Leviticus we will find laws dealing with morals and ethics. These are laws that still apply to this day, although even these are fulfilled through faith in Christ by loving God and loving our neighbor. (Romans 13:10; Galatians 5:14) They are true and right guidelines for life given by our Father and Creator. Some examples of moral law might be laws against murder, child sacrifice, dishonoring parents, stealing, lying, coveting or sexual sin.

THE THREE USES OF THE LAW

As Christians today, we live under a new covenant. Because we live under the new covenant, some readers tend to think, then, that the old covenant of the Old Testament is entirely obsolete. In fact, the New Testament says in Hebrews 10:1 that the old law could not make us perfect. It did not have the ability to save us. Since this is the case, the purpose of the old law sometimes becomes confusing. In his book *Institutes of the Christian Religion*, John Calvin provides a look into what we know as the "three uses of the law."[1] Let's look at each one.

FIRST USE OF THE LAW
MIRROR

One major purpose of the law is to show us the absolute holiness of God. God shows us His standards for living a holy life. And when we hold up the law like a mirror to our own lives, we are able to see just how utterly short we all fall. Romans 3:20 says, *"through the law comes knowledge of sin,"* and in Romans 7:7d, Paul writes, *"if it had not been for the law, I would not have known sin."* The law shows us that we are sinners, and it gives us a reason to cry out to God and to marvel at His mercy and grace.

SECOND USE OF THE LAW
RESTRAINT

Another purpose of the old law was to provide civil order. It was meant to keep evil in check. Punishments were included to inhibit lawlessness. Even Romans 13:4b says, *"if you do wrong, be afraid ..."* None of us would want to live in a world where there was no law or civil order — where evil went unpunished and everyone could do as they pleased. Even as Christians today, part of our hope is in knowing that someday God will right all wrongs, and evil will be punished. (Revelation 21:8)

THIRD USE OF THE LAW
SANCTIFICATION

The final purpose of the law is meant to guide us toward holiness. The law does not save us, but it can help sanctify us. This means I will not receive God's salvation by keeping the Ten Commandments (because I could never do so perfectly), but after I have received God's salvation through the grace of Jesus and His sacrifice, now I can look to the Ten Commandments to see how I can better live in a way that pleases Him. I can study the law to see God's heart (for example, so many of the laws of Leviticus were to protect the vulnerable and weak), and I can put that heart into practice in my own life as I desire more and more to look like my Father.

WHAT YOU HAVE TO LOOK FORWARD TO IN THIS LEVITICUS STUDY GUIDE

In addition to the background information and daily questions for studying Leviticus, we have included several elements to deepen your study along the way.

CHARTS AND GRAPHS

As a visual learner, I love a good chart or graph! Within this guide, you will find several charts to help you see the material from Leviticus in a short and organized way. Designed throughout the guide, look for a table comparing the five sacrifices, a diagram of the early tabernacle and a chart laying out the Holy Feasts.

ESPECIALLY HARD (BUT HOLY) SECTIONS

One of the biggest concerns people sometimes bring to Leviticus is that it is "hard." They say it is hard to read, hard to understand and honestly hard to accept. Indeed, there are several parts that seem to grate against the conscience and minds of modern-day, New Testament believers. Thankfully, we do not have to be left in the dark on how we approach these sections. In this guide, we will tackle together six especially hard (but holy, nonetheless) topics from Leviticus. They are:

- Menstruation
- Homosexuality
- Capital Punishment
- People With Disabilities
- Slavery
- Prosperity Gospel

WEEKEND REFLECTIONS

We will wrap up each week with a deeper study of a section we read that week. In many instances, we will discover other places in the Bible where we see a particular law put into action. Every Weekend Reflection will help us apply the truth behind the law to our lives today.

IN CASE YOU WERE WONDERING

Wrapping up our study guide, you will find 10 verses from Leviticus that maybe you have heard somewhere before. Our First 5 team has written a quick study on each verse to take you even deeper into the meaning, context or Hebrew origins. This is your chance to get into the fun details of Scripture and have an even richer understanding and appreciation of God's Word the next time you hear a verse used.

Dear parents or guardians: While God's Word is perfect and true, there are certain topics addressed in Leviticus that deal with adult content and might not be suitable for children. We recommend parental guidance throughout the study.

MAJOR MOMENTS

WEEK 1

LEVITICUS 1:1-17 — *Burnt offerings represented total commitment to God.*
LEVITICUS 2:1-16 — *Grain offerings were acts of worship.*
LEVITICUS 3:1-17 — *The peace offering represented peace with God and man.*
LEVITICUS 4:1-21 — *The greater the leadership, the greater the consequences of sin.*
LEVITICUS 4:22-35 — *Sin offerings were established to make atonement.*

WEEK 2

LEVITICUS 5:1-13 — *Atonement for sin required confession and a mediator.*
LEVITICUS 5:14-6:7 — *Guilt offerings required restitution.*
LEVITICUS 6:8-7:10 — *God laid out precise instructions for His priests.*
LEVITICUS 7:11-38 — *The sacrificial system showed the holy, costly work of atonement.*
LEVITICUS 8:1-36 — *Aaron and his sons were set apart as priests.*

WEEK 3

LEVITICUS 9:1-24 — *The glory of the Lord appeared at the inaugural worship service.*
LEVITICUS 10:1-20 — *A disrespectful attitude toward God had serious consequences.*
LEVITICUS 11:1-47 — *The distinction between clean and unclean animals was a constant reminder of holiness to God's people.*
LEVITICUS 12:1-8 — *While childbirth made a woman unclean, God made a way for her to return to worship.*
LEVITICUS 13:1-59 — *Those with unclean skin afflictions lived outside the camp to preserve the health of the whole.*

WEEK 4

LEVITICUS 14:1-57 — *God provided a way for the unclean to be declared clean again.*
LEVITICUS 15:1-33 — *God's laws on bodily discharge taught about sex.*
LEVITICUS 16:1-34 — *The Day of Atonement was the only time the high priest could enter the Holy Place and make full atonement.*
LEVITICUS 17:1-9 — *Sacrifices could only be made before the tabernacle.*
LEVITICUS 17:10-16 — *Blood represents life.*

WEEK 5

LEVITICUS 18:1-30 — *God made rules for His creation regarding sexual relations.*
LEVITICUS 19:1-8 — *God commanded holiness.*
LEVITICUS 19:9-18 — *God commanded holiness through loving our neighbor.*
LEVITICUS 19:19-37 — *God's statutes guided His people in holy living.*
LEVITICUS 20:1-9 — *Disobedience had severe consequences.*

WEEK 6

LEVITICUS 20:10-21 — *Sexual sins carried especially severe consequences.*
LEVITICUS 20:22-27 — *Holiness required separation.*
LEVITICUS 21:1-22:16 — *Priests were called to a higher standard.*
LEVITICUS 22:17-33 — *The quality of the offering mattered.*
LEVITICUS 23:1-8 — *God established holy days.*

WEEK 7

LEVITICUS 23:9-25 — *God ordained the Feasts of the Firstfruits, Weeks and Trumpets.*
LEVITICUS 23:26-32 — *The Day of Atonement was to be treated seriously.*
LEVITICUS 23:33-44 — *The Feast of Booths was about rejoicing before the Lord.*
LEVITICUS 24:1-9 — *The light and the loaves represented God's continual presence.*
LEVITICUS 24:10-23 — *The law established that punishments should fit the crime.*

WEEK 8

LEVITICUS 25:1-22 — *The Sabbath and Jubilee years established social, economic and theological principles.*
LEVITICUS 25:23-34 — *God provided a way for those who fell on hard times.*
LEVITICUS 25:35-55 — *Israelites were only to be servants of God.*
LEVITICUS 26:1-46 — *God set conditions for His blessings and punishment.*
LEVITICUS 27:1-34 — *God kept His word, and He expected His people to do the same.*

WEEK 1

DAY 1

Leviticus 1:1-17

BURNT OFFERINGS REPRESENTED TOTAL COMMITMENT TO GOD.

The book of Leviticus starts with *"The LORD called Moses ..."* (Leviticus 1:1). A variation of this phrase occurs 38 times in Leviticus. Another 18 times we see the statement that the Lord *"commanded Moses."* This means a total of 56 times in Leviticus we are told that the Lord directly spoke to His people. [1] This book is filled with words directly from God's mouth. That makes the study of Leviticus so very important.

Take a moment, as we begin this study, to write a short prayer acknowledging that this book is holy and inspired. Ask the Lord to use His Word to speak to your heart through this study.

Fill in the blanks from verse 2:

"... WHEN ANY ONE OF YOU ______________ AN OFFERING TO THE LORD, YOU SHALL ______________ YOUR OFFERING OF LIVESTOCK FROM THE HERD OR FROM THE FLOCK."

The ESV translation of the Hebrew word for "bring" more fully means "to come, to approach, to be close," or to draw near. [2] The heart of God is to draw a sinful people near to Him again. When the first man and woman hid in the garden after their sin, God sought them out and called for them. During the time the words of Leviticus were given, the people God had rescued from Egypt had already tried to make an idol to worship. Yet God never stopped pursuing sinful people to draw them near to Him again.

How does Romans 5:8 show us that this is still the case for us today?

Let's take a look at the first of the five offerings: **the burnt offering.**

Leviticus 1:3 and 1:10 say the animal sacrificed must be without what?

What do we learn in 1 Peter 1:19?

According to Leviticus 1:9, how much of the sacrifice was burned?

Look ahead at Leviticus 7:8. What did the priests receive for performing the sacrifice?

The burnt offering was about complete and total commitment to God. Besides the hide, the fire consumed all of the animal to represent this level of commitment to God. The sacrifice had to be without blemish because it represented giving our very best to God.

Read the account from Malachi 1:6-8. How does God feel when we offer Him less than our very best?

Within the book of Leviticus we have what we call "rituals." A ritual is a ceremonial or customary practice. Today people sometimes think rituals are meaningless or empty. And perhaps if they are done without thought, they can be. But as Allan Moseley says in *Exalting Jesus in Leviticus*, "The real meaning of a ritual is what is in a person's heart when he observes it." [3]

Read Psalm 51:16. Interestingly, what does this verse say God is not pleased with?

Now read Psalm 51:17. What does God desire instead?

Let's end with a look at one final phrasing.

Leviticus 1:9, 1:13 and 1:17 all end with what six-word phrase?

How does this relate to Ephesians 5:2?

If the burnt offering is about total commitment and giving our very best to God, what can we learn from Ephesians 5:2 about how to do so? What about Romans 12:1-2?

DAY 2

Leviticus 2:1-16

GRAIN OFFERINGS WERE ACTS OF WORSHIP.

Yesterday we talked about how the sacrificial system established here in Leviticus was God's invitation to His people to draw near to Him. We draw near to God for love and forgiveness, but we also become closer to Him in worship. The grain offering from today's reading was an offering of worship.

The Hebrew word for "grain offering" here is *min-hah. Min-hah* is also used several other times in the Old Testament, but in those situations, it is in reference to a gift or a **tribute** given to the ruling king. (For example, see 2 Samuel 8:2 and 8:6.) *Min-hah* was meant for a king.

What might this added definition remind you about God?

Grain was a food staple, and grain or bread is symbolic of provision in the Bible. Perhaps that is why Jesus used this symbol in Matthew 6:11 when teaching the Lord's Prayer.

What did Jesus teach us to pray in Matthew 6:11?

The grain offering was one way the people actively remembered where their provisions came from and was a way to say "thanks."

What does James 1:17 remind us as well?

The act of bringing grain and offering it to the Lord was a form of worship where the people were reminded of who cared for them, how blessed they were and how they could give back. Each part of this grain offering is packed with information to study.

Leviticus 2:1 says the *"offering shall be of"* what? (This particular kind of flour came from the inner kernel of the wheat and received multiple grindings, making it the most expensive type of flour.)

Leviticus 2:2 says to pour oil and to add what particular spice to the flour? (These were also quite expensive.)

What do these ingredients tell us about this offering?

We should always give the best of what we have, to the best of our ability, but this does not mean those who did not have money could not worship God. God always made a way for the poor to join in worship as well, for God's concern was for the heart. In this particular instance, if a person could not afford frankincense, there was something else they could offer.

Read Leviticus 2:4-7. What could be done and offered without frankincense?

Giving in worship is not just about giving money. It can also mean giving of one's time. When was the last time you gave either time or money as an act of worship to the Lord?

Leviticus 2:11-13 tells us of things that could and could not be added to the grain offering.

What two things could not be added? (v. 11)

What *must* be added? (v. 13)

Yeast was a common metaphor for corruption. The leavening process involves fermentation, which is a form of decay. Decay is a form of death. Honey can also be fermented, which is perhaps why it is listed in verse 11.

Read 1 Corinthians 5:8. Paul uses the metaphor of leavening to describe celebrating the sacrifice of Jesus. According to this verse, what is the leaven? And what is the unleavened bread?

In the ancient Near East, salt was a symbol for covenant. It was Israel's reminder that they had a relationship with God, and He with them. Salt was also a preservative. This reminded them that this relationship would persevere and be ongoing.

In Matthew 5:13a, Jesus calls us the *"salt of the earth."* As salt, we are to show the world God's covenant and preservation. What is one practical way you can be salt this week (i.e. in your relationships, speech, etc.)?

Let's look at one final note on this grain offering of worship. Leviticus 2:2-3 says only a handful of the grain offering was burned on the altar.

What happened to the rest of the grain offering?

What might this teach us about how we worship God?

DAY 3

Leviticus 3:1-17

THE PEACE OFFERING REPRESENTED PEACE WITH GOD AND MAN.

Today we look at the third offering, which is the peace offering. Other translations of the Bible sometimes refer to this as the "fellowship offering." The Hebrew word used here is a root word of *shalom*, which often means peace. Both "peace" and "fellowship" are good words to describe this offering.

According to Leviticus 3:1, 3:6 and 3:12, what three animals could be offered for the peace offering?

If we look ahead for a moment, Leviticus 7:11-36 gives more details into the peace offering. According to Leviticus 7:15, what could the person who offered the sacrifice do?

The peace offering is the only offering where the worshipper (not just the priest) also shared in the eating of the sacrifice. The peace offering was about joy and celebration. The food was shared with loved ones. How often it seems that food and fellowship go together!

Read the account of Solomon dedicating the temple in 1 Kings 8:62-65. How many animals were given for the peace offering? This resulted in a massive amount of food that was used for what in verse 65?

In your opinion, why might food and fellowship be so closely linked?

In the ancient Near East, eating together signified friends or allies. And indeed, God's love and care was the best reason to celebrate peace among men. But even more than peace between people, the peace offering was about celebrating peace with God. Because of the covenant God had made, and because He allowed for atonement for sin so people could draw near Him once again, there could be fellowship with God. Let's take a look at some of the specifics given in the text and see what they have to teach us about God.

In Leviticus 3:3, 3:9 and 3:14-15, the priests are told to offer what as a food offering to the Lord?

In ancient Israel, the "fat" (*heleb*) represented the very best part of the animal.[1] Given the context, what does giving the "fat" of the sacrifice to God teach us?

In Leviticus 3:4, 3:10 and 3:15, the people are commanded to specifically remove from the animal and burn on the altar the two kidneys with the fat, along with the what?

The Canaanites, people of an ancient pagan culture that was quite influential during this time period, often used animal livers to perform a type of divination or fortune-telling. The One True God wanted His people to have nothing to do with such practices. What might burning the liver have signified to the Israelite people?

In Leviticus 3:2, 3:8 and 3:13, what was sprinkled around the sides of the altar?

We, too, have a reason to celebrate. We truly have peace with God, and it was made possible by Jesus. According to Colossians 1:20, Jesus made peace with God possible by what?

To end today, look over what you have learned in this chapter.

What does today's study of the peace offering have to teach us about both peace with God and fellowship with others?

DAY 4

Leviticus 4:1-21

THE GREATER THE LEADERSHIP, THE GREATER THE CONSEQUENCES OF SIN.

Today we'll begin by looking at sin offerings. We will break down this section into three days to see each part in full. Today's section deals specifically with sin offerings for priests and the whole congregation.

In these sin offerings, one word keeps showing up. Fill in the blank using Leviticus 4:2:

"SPEAK TO THE PEOPLE OF ISRAEL, SAYING, IF ANYONE SINS ______________ IN ANY OF THE LORD'S COMMANDMENTS ABOUT THINGS NOT TO BE DONE, AND DOES ANY ONE OF THEM ..."

Maybe people didn't know they weren't supposed to do something. There was an ignorance of the law. Other times perhaps they were negligent, accidentally stumbling into something they shouldn't have. They didn't *mean* to break the law. Often, we can use such reasons as an excuse for our sin. But notice here in Leviticus, even unintentional sin is still considered sin.

Read Psalm 19:12. David asked the Lord to declare him innocent, or forgive him, from what? This is in contrast to the kind of sins mentioned in the next verse. Feel free to check out other translations to compare.

Take a moment to read Psalm 139:23-24. Write a short prayer using this psalm. Ask God to reveal any hidden or unintentional sins so that you, too, can walk in the way everlasting.

As we examine today's text concerning the sin offerings of priests and the congregation, let's take a few notes.

What animal was to be offered? (Leviticus 4:3, 4:14)

Take a sneak peek up ahead. What animal were civic leaders to offer? (v. 23) And how about common people? (v. 28)

Which of these animals was greater in terms of size and cost?

Now let's look at the sprinkling of the blood. For the priests' and the congregation's sins, what was done with the blood? Look at the two kinds of altars. (vv. 6-7, 17-18)

Look ahead again. For civic leaders and common people, where was the blood put? Look at the two kinds of altars. (vv. 25, 30)

Look at the diagram of the tabernacle. Where is the altar of incense and the veil compared to the bronze altar used for burnt offerings? Which is further away from the entrance to the tabernacle?

What does this teach us about leadership? Why might this be the case?

Let's end today looking at one final note on the sin offering.

While some of the offering was burned on the altar, where was the flesh of the bull taken and burned? (vv. 11-12, 21)

Read the beautiful words of Hebrews 13:11-13. Write down what you learn.

THE TABERNACLE

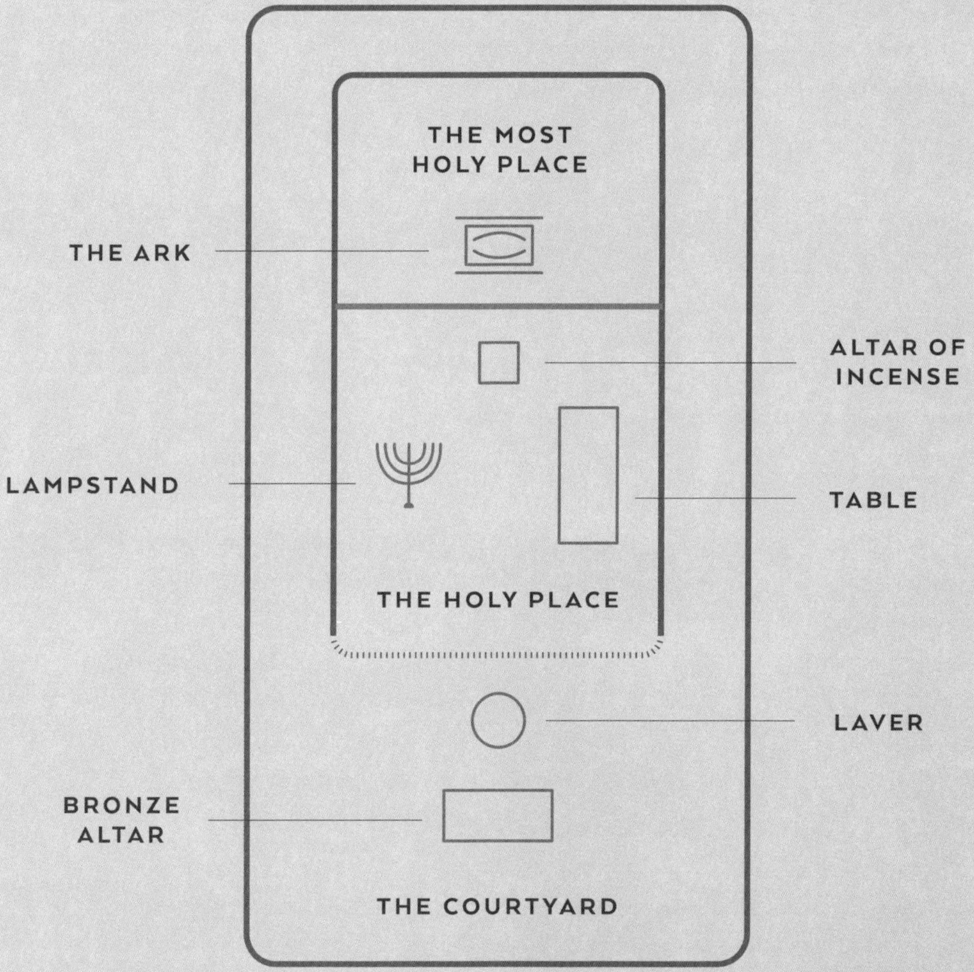

DAY 5

Leviticus 4:22-35

SIN OFFERINGS WERE ESTABLISHED TO MAKE ATONEMENT.

Yesterday we looked at the sin offerings for priests and the congregation as a whole. We also glanced at today's reading, which focuses on the sin offerings of civic leaders and common people. From what we read, we learned that the greater the leadership role, the higher the consequences were for sin. In today's reading, we'll see that even lay leaders are held to a higher standard than people who aren't in leadership positions.

What kind of goat did leaders have to offer? (v. 23)

What kind of goat or lamb could common people offer (which was less expensive)? (vv. 28, 32)

Leadership comes with responsibility. And while Matthew 18:6 refers to those who lead children astray, I believe it can also apply to leadership generally. What does this verse say, and how does it apply here?

One phrase is often repeated in today's text. It is crucial for us to grasp the full meaning.

Read Leviticus 4:26, 4:31 and 4:35. Fill in the blanks:

"SO THE PRIEST SHALL MAKE ________________ FOR HIM FOR HIS SIN, AND HE SHALL BE ______________." (V. 26B)

The Hebrew word for "atone," *kaphar*, means covering. It could be a covering to hide, or it could be used as in "covering for someone." [1]

Using this definition, what provides the "covering" for sin in Leviticus 4?

In English, the word "atone" has at its root the idea of two estranged parties being made "at-one" with each other. [2]

Using this definition, what two estranged parties are made "at-one" in Leviticus 4?

Using what you have learned, write a definition for atonement in your own words.

If blood makes you squeamish, Leviticus might be difficult to read. Sacrifices were a bloody, messy business. What is the deal with all of this blood anyway?

Leviticus 17:14 sheds some light on this. Write word-for-word the first sentence of this verse.

Now, read Romans 6:23. What is the cost — the price — of sin?

Sin = Death. Blood = Life. What does Hebrews 9:22 tell us?

Let's end on one verse that so perfectly sums up today. Read 1 Peter 2:24.

How does this verse show us atonement?

How does this verse show us sin is death, and blood is life?

Take a moment to write a prayer of gratitude to Jesus for everything His sacrifice meant.

Weekend Reflection

WEEK 1

During our study of Leviticus, we are going to use the weekends to examine further an area of Leviticus and how the principles behind the law are still relevant to us today.

For Week 1, let's take a deeper look into the grain offering we studied in Chapter 2. Remember the grain offering was given from "fine flour." This was from the best part of the grain, ground multiple times. But let's take just a moment to consider the context of the situation in Leviticus.

The laws of Leviticus were given to Moses only shortly after the people had left Egypt. This meant their status at the time was "nomad." They wandered through the wilderness. They did not have land, nor were they growing crops. So where did this special flour come from?

Some people have speculated that these first grain offerings had to have come from the seed grain the Israelites were planning to plant once they arrived in the promised land.[1] That seed grain would have been their hope for a better future. Yet instead of holding on to what they had for themselves, they offered the best portions of it to God because they knew the One who held their future. They trusted in the Lord to provide for them, to take care of them, to make a way.

When was the last time we poured ourselves out before the Lord, whether our resources, time, energy, heart, soul, mind or emotion, and gave so much away that we had to completely trust Him to provide? Philippians 4:19 says God *"will supply every need of yours according to his riches in glory in Christ Jesus."* In fact, God *"is able to do far more abundantly than all that we ask or think"* (Ephesians 3:20). His power is at work within us and He will not fail.

So go ahead and open your hand. Give God those seeds you are so desperately trying to grasp. And trust Him to grow the crop you need.

WEEK 2

DAY 6

Leviticus 5:1-13

ATONEMENT FOR SIN REQUIRED CONFESSION AND A MEDIATOR.

Today we will wrap up our look into the sin offering. We learned how the sin offering affected priests and the group as a whole, and how it affected civic leaders and common people. Today we'll look at three specific sins God warned them against. These are relevant today because they have much to teach us about the heart of God.

According to Leviticus 5:1, what was the first sin mentioned?

Sometimes we are silent because of fear, sometimes because of indifference. But not stepping up to the cause of justice is the same as promoting injustice.

In what areas have you seen or been made aware of injustice lately? How can you speak up for what is right?

What does this teach us about the heart of God?

According to Leviticus 5:2-3, what is the second sin mentioned?

When God gave His law, He commanded that some things be considered "unclean." Now, to be ritually unclean was not a sin. To be unclean simply meant one could not participate in religious rites and rituals until one was cleansed. For this, God laid out protocols for what to do when a person became unclean. (See Leviticus 11 for example.)

According to Leviticus 5:2-3, the person could unknowingly become unclean, and if they did not follow the proper procedures to be clean, they would break God's law. This also meant they would unknowingly spread the contamination, but carelessness is not an excuse. These laws were not to be taken flippantly.

What part of God's Word have you not been diligent to follow?

What do verses 2-3 teach us about the heart of God?

What sin is mentioned in Leviticus 5:4?

Ecclesiastes 5:2a says, *"Be not rash with your mouth, nor let your heart be hasty to utter a word before God ..."*

Deuteronomy 23:23 says, *"You shall be careful to do what has passed your lips ..."*

As followers of God, we are to be people who **keep our word**.

What promises have you made that you have delayed in following through with? What is something you said you would do that still needs to be done?

What does Leviticus 5:4 teach us about the heart of God?

As we have looked at the sin offering and everything that it entailed, perhaps it makes us think of our own sin. During this time in the old covenant, sacrifices were required. And while that may no longer seem relevant to us today, we do have some things in common when it comes to dealing with our sin.

What is a key part of sin offerings mentioned in Leviticus 5:5?

What does 1 John 1:8-9 teach us today?

What animals are mentioned in Leviticus 5:6?

What does Hebrews 10:4 say?

Go on down and read Hebrews 10:8-10. What offering does sanctify us?

Finally, on Day 5, we looked specifically at the word "atonement." We see this word again in the same phrasing in today's reading, but today, let's focus on a different word. Fill in the blank using Leviticus 5:6, 5:10 and 5:13:

"AND THE ______________ SHALL MAKE ATONEMENT FOR HIM FOR HIS SIN."

The priest was the mediator. He went between the sinner and God, bringing the sacrifice before the Lord and asking forgiveness on behalf of the sinner. The truth is, we still need a mediator today. What does 1 Timothy 2:5 say about this?

DAY 7

Leviticus 5:14-6:7

GUILT OFFERINGS REQUIRED RESTITUTION.

We have looked closer at burnt offerings, grain offerings, peace offerings and sin offerings. Today we will look at the last of the five offerings: the guilt offering. Some scholars use the term "trespass offering" or "reparation offering." The guilt offering differs from the sin offering in that some kind of reparation needed to be offered to make things right. Let's look at the three main types of sin covered by the guilt offering.

SIN AGAINST THE HOLY THINGS

To begin, let's examine the serious nature of these offenses. Leviticus 5:15 calls this sin, as well as the sin listed in 6:2, a *"breach of faith."*

What terms does Numbers 5:12 use to refer to the act of adultery? (ESV)

Adultery meant breaking the marriage covenant. These sins listed in Leviticus 5 broke the Lord's covenant. The first sin listed is to sin against *"the holy things of the LORD"* (Leviticus 5:15).

Look back at Leviticus 2:3. What was one thing that was considered a "holy" thing of the Lord?

And also according to Leviticus 2:3, who were these holy things meant for?

To take from the holy things was not only a sin against God, but it also took from the priests' portion. It makes sense, then, why restitution for taking these things or defiling them had to be paid to whom, according to Leviticus 5:16?

UNKNOWN SINS

The next section (Leviticus 5:17-19) is interesting. Within this section of the guilt offering, we see no mention of any kind of restitution. However, this is probably because the person didn't actually know what to ask forgiveness for or how to make it right. This is about unknown sins — that nagging sense of guilt that won't go away, but we don't know why. Research has found that accidentally committing a sin and not knowing you had done so was a common fear, not only of the ancient Israelites but of others in the ancient Near East as well. [1]

Has there ever been a time where you worried about accidentally messing up and making God angry?

1 John 1:9 teaches us that God can

"FORGIVE US ... FROM ____________ UNRIGHTEOUSNESS."

TAKING FROM OUR NEIGHBOR

While the first section dealt with stealing from God (and His priests), this final section is about taking from our neighbors.

What sins against a neighbor are found in Leviticus 6:1-5 (ESV)?

1. "IF ANYONE SINS AND COMMITS A BREACH OF FAITH AGAINST THE LORD BY DECEIVING HIS NEIGHBOR IN A MATTER OF ______________ OR ________________ ..." (V. 2)

2. "OR THROUGH ________________________ ..." (V. 2)

3. "OR IF HE HAS ________________________ HIS NEIGHBOR..." (V. 2)

4. "OR HAS FOUND SOMETHING ____________________ AND __________________ ABOUT IT, __________________ __________________ ..." (V. 3)

According to verse 5, this person was to restore it in full and add what?

What example do we have of restitution in Luke 19:8-9?

I think the term "guilt offering" is telling. Guilt leads (hopefully) to repentance. Repentance leads to restitution. As children of God, we do more than say, "Oops. Sorry." We go out of our way to make it right.

When was the last time you had to apologize to someone? What did you do to help make it right?

What does this teach us about the heart of God?

FIVE SACRIFICES OF LEVITICUS

NAME	GIFT	WORSHIPER'S WORK	PRIEST'S WORK	GOD'S PORTION	WORSHIPER'S PORTION	PRIEST'S PORTION	ANCIENT MEANING	MEANING IN JESUS
BURNT OFFERING	Male cow, male sheep or goat, dove or pigeon	Bring to tabernacle, lay hands on, kill, skin, wash, give to priest	Catch blood and sprinkle on altar, burn everything on altar	Everything except for skin	None	Skin	Complete and total dedication	Christ gave Himself as a complete burnt offering. (Ephesians 5:2; Isaiah 53:7; Mark 12:33)
GRAIN OFFERING	Fine flour or grain with oil, salt and frankincense (if it could be afforded), no leaven or honey	Finely grind grain (offering could be baked without frankincense)	Put handful of flour and all frankincense on altar	The handful of flour and all the frankincense	None	The rest that was not given to the Lord	Thanksgiving for God's provision, giving back to God	Christ is the Bread of Life. We are to take and eat, remembering His body. (John 6:35; Luke 22:19)

NAME	GIFT	WORSHIPER'S WORK	PRIEST'S WORK	GOD'S PORTION	WORSHIPER'S PORTION	PRIEST'S PORTION	ANCIENT MEANING	MEANING IN JESUS
PEACE OFFERING	Cow, lamb, goat – male or female — along with loaves of bread and oil	Bring to tabernacle, lay hands on, kill, take out fat, kidneys and liver	Catch blood, sprinkle at altar, wave breast and right thigh before God	The fat, kidneys and liver plus one loaf bread	Everything not burned or given to the priest	The breast and right thigh waved before God, plus remaining bread	Fellowship and communion with God and each other	Christ is our peace offering, bringing us into communion. (Romans 5:1; Colossians 1:20)
SIN OFFERING	Bull for priest or nation, male goat for leaders, female goat or lamb (or two doves/pigeons or tenth ephah of flour) for all others	Same as peace offering	If for the nation or priest, sprinkle blood before veil and on horns of altar; if for others, smear blood on horns of altar and pour the rest at base	The fat, kidneys and liver burned on the altar; the head, legs, entrails and dung burned outside of camp	None	All that remained of the meat	Forgiveness of sin	Christ is our sin offering. (2 Corinthians 5:21; 1 Peter 2:24)
GUILT OFFERING	Ram (plus restitution)	Same as peace and sin offerings	Smear blood on horns of altar and pour the rest at base of altar	The fat, kidneys and liver	Everything that wasn't burned on the altar	Everything that wasn't burned on the altar	Restitution for sin	Christ is our guilt offering. (Colossians 2:13-14; 2 Corinthians 5:19)

DAY 8

Leviticus 6:8-7:10

GOD LAID OUT PRECISE INSTRUCTIONS FOR HIS PRIESTS.

So far in our study of Leviticus, we have studied the five major sacrifices that were to be offered to the Lord. We can see how this would have been a full-time job for those who were priests. And God wanted to carefully lay out His instructions so that the expectations were clear up front.

Think of a time when you were asked to do a job (or volunteered to do one) and you were not given good instructions. How did that make you feel? How did that task go?

Today we'll look at the priests' additional specific instructions for four of the five offerings. Tomorrow we'll look at the fifth.

BURNT OFFERINGS

Let's do a quick review of burnt offerings. Look back at Leviticus 1:9. How much of the burnt offering was to be put on the fire?

This would have made for a lot of ash, so part of today's reading is the practical aspect of what to do with that ash. But notice the changing of the clothes in Leviticus 6:10-11. To come near the altar, the priest had to wear what?

Growing up, on Sunday mornings I had to put on my "church dress." It was a cultural ritual that was supposed to show we took the effort to look our best for the Lord's house. Men remove their caps or hats during prayer for the same reason. It is a sign of respect. Can you think of other "rituals" we perform today as signs of respect?

Especially highlighted in this section of Scripture is the fact that the fire of the altar was to be kept burning continually. This represented so many things. What did fire represent in Deuteronomy 4:24?

One of my favorite smells in the winter is that of a wood-burning fireplace. It floods me with memories of Christmas at home growing up — keeping warm by the fire. The constant fire from the altar would have sent the smell throughout the camp. It was a reminder to the people of God's forgiveness and His constant presence. As Allan Mosely puts it, "God is never 'Closed for Business.'"[1] What does the continual fire upon the altar remind you about God?

GRAIN OFFERINGS

Here the priests receive instructions on the grain offerings. Let's compare two sections and see what we learn ...

According to Leviticus 6:16, after a handful was burned on the fire, what became of the rest of the grain offerings?

The priests were doing the Lord's work. As compensation, they were allowed to eat some of the grain offering. But look at the contrast in verses 20–23.

In verse 20, the priests were commanded to make their own grain offering. How much of this could they eat? (v. 23)

Priests did an important job, and they were taken care of. Yet the Lord also wanted them to be reminded they were exactly like everyone else; they, too, were in desperate need of God, and they, too, needed to honor and worship Him.

Read Romans 12:3. Why might we also need this kind of reminder in our own lives today?

SIN OFFERINGS

Leviticus 6:24-30 gives instructions for sin offerings.

Underline every time you see the word "holy." How many did you find?

Dealing with sin was a holy matter. It was to be taken seriously. The blood that was spilled had been a life given in exchange for another. This meant everything the blood touched was affected. Stained clothes had to be washed in holy places. Clay pots were porous and might have absorbed some of the blood; they couldn't have been washed clean of it, so they had to be broken. Blood was not to be treated lightly. Atonement is a holy and serious business.

Think about the day you made the decision to accept Christ's sacrifice on your behalf. What about that experience would you consider holy?

GUILT OFFERING

Once again, the guilt offering stresses the importance of following some very specific instructions. For our study today, let's focus on Leviticus 7:7-10.

Write down what the priests received from each of the offerings:

- Guilt offering (v. 7): ______________________
- Burnt offering (v. 8) : ______________________
- Grain offering that is baked (v. 9): ______________________
- Grain offering that is mixed with oil or dry (v. 10): ______________________

Guilt offerings were one of the built-in ways that God used to provide for the priests dedicated to doing His work. What does 1 Corinthians 9:13-14 say about ministers both then and now?

Read Galatians 6:6. What is one way that you can personally reach out to meet the needs of those who teach, pastor or guide you spiritually?

DAY 9

Leviticus 7:11-38

THE SACRIFICIAL SYSTEM SHOWED THE HOLY, COSTLY WORK OF ATONEMENT.

Yesterday we looked at the instructions for the priests for four of the five offerings. Much of today's reading focuses on the peace offering but also wraps it all together. By the end of today, we will see how the sacrificial system was designed for a purpose that is so very relevant to us as Christians today.

Let's start down in Leviticus 7:19-21.

What would you say is the overall subject of these verses?

The laws governing what was clean and unclean might seem random. However, these verses were not necessarily about the unclean "thing." Things themselves are not inherently good or bad. In fact, let's look at the New Testament.

Read Acts 10:9-16. According to this account, what makes an item clean or unclean?

The heart behind the laws of cleanliness had everything to do with our own heart problem. Things did not defile the people; disobedience to God defiled them. God said, "Don't." But they, and we, still do. Our hearts have rebelled against God's good ways from the beginning. Yet, still, God calls His people to live differently, according to His plan.

Next let's look into Leviticus 7:22-27.

According to these verses, people were not allowed to do what?

Remember, the priest laid the fat of the offerings upon the altar to God as part of the sacrifice for the people's sin and guilt. The priest then sprinkled, smeared and poured the blood on the altar as the cost for atonement. Everything to do with the atonement of sins should be treated with respect.

Studying even deeper, Leviticus 7:26 says, *"you shall eat no blood whatever ..."*

What did Jesus say in John 6:56 that would have been truly shocking for a Jew?

In Leviticus 17:11, we learn that the people were taught *"the life of the flesh is in the blood."* Yet how does Jesus qualify this saying in John 6:63?

Therefore, when Jesus says to drink His blood, He is using this as a symbol that we should take in His what?

Finally, Leviticus 7:37 gives us the wrap-up for the five offerings that were to be performed. Let's take a quick look at each one again and compare it to Jesus. Look up the New Testament verses and answer the questions.

THE OLD TESTAMENT OFFERING	WHAT IT SYMBOLIZED	HOW JESUS FULFILLED IT
BURNT OFFERING (also known as a Whole Offering)	Complete and total devotion, giving one's all	Philippians 2:7-8 says Jesus did what? How? What did Jesus say about burnt offerings in Mark 12:33?
GRAIN OFFERING (also known as a First Fruits Offering)	Thanksgiving and trust for provision	In Luke 22:42, who does Jesus trust with His own life? How are we like the grain or first fruits offerings, according to James 1:18?
PEACE OFFERING (also known as an Offering of Well-Being — in addition, Praise, Vow and Freewill offerings fell in this category)	Peace and fellowship with God	In Colossians 1:20, Jesus' blood makes what? Passover was part of a peace offering. Jesus is our Passover lamb. (1 Corinthians 5:7)

THE OLD TESTAMENT OFFERING	WHAT IT SYMBOLIZED	HOW JESUS FULFILLED IT
SIN OFFERING (also known as a Purification Offering)	Atonement, covering of sin	In 1 John 4:10, Jesus became the what? (Also see John 1:29.)
GUILT OFFERING (also known as a Reparation Offering)	Restitution for the debt sin caused	Read Isaiah 53:10 and note the type of offering mentioned. Now read Colossians 2:13-14. God has now done what? How?

The ultimate goal of every single Old Testament offering was to point us to the life and death of Jesus Christ. Thank You, Jesus, for everything that Your sacrifice truly entailed!

DAY 10

Leviticus 8:1-36

AARON AND HIS SONS WERE SET APART AS PRIESTS.

Now that the rules for the offerings were established, the next line of business was to establish the priesthood that would perform these all-important tasks. Today we study the ceremony that essentially ordained Aaron and his sons as priests.

To help make this passage relatable to today, list different ceremonies you have witnessed or been a part of. Describe the atmosphere surrounding these ceremonies.

The ceremony that established the Jewish priesthood took place in seven parts.

1. PREPARATION (Leviticus 8:1-4)

According to these verses, Moses had to gather all the needed materials, as well as do what in verse 3? Why might this have been important?

2. WASHING AND CLOTHES FOR AARON (vv. 5-9)

A common ritual and symbol for purification was washing with water. What do we have that is similar in 1 Peter 3:21?

Notice the elaborate clothing set aside for Aaron as the high priest. These garments set him apart from the other priests. Look back at the ceremonies you wrote down. In what ways do outward items set people apart in these ceremonies as well?

Notice the words used to describe the clothing. Robes often indicated royalty, as did crowns. This is interesting because priests were not royalty in the Old Testament. There was a clear distinction. That is, until Jesus came along. Even the clothing was a foreshadowing of what was to come. What does Hebrews 4:14 call Jesus? What about 1 Timothy 6:14-15?

3. ANOINTING OF THE TABERNACLE AND CLOTHES FOR OTHER PRIESTS (vv. 10-13)

Oil was used for anointing. Oil is a common biblical symbol for something else you might be familiar with. What did Jesus say He was anointed by in Luke 4:18?

The other priests, while not as decorated as the high priest, were still specially clothed. What does Galatians 3:27 say for us?

4. SIN OFFERING (vv. 14-17)

This may seem obvious, but it is important to mention because this was a big weakness of the old covenant system (a weakness that Jesus as Great High Priest corrected in the new covenant): A sin offering was given to atone for sin.

So if the high priest (Aaron) and his sons were offering a sin offering, what did this suggest about them? And according to Hebrews 7:26-27, what made Jesus different?

5. BURNT OFFERING (vv. 18-21)

Remember, a burnt offering represented complete dedication of oneself to God.

6. ORDINATION OFFERING (vv. 22-29)

Similar to a peace offering, this offering confirmed the covenant between God and the priests. It joined these two estranged parties (God and sinful men) in an agreement. What unique outward symbol was done to Aaron and his sons to show their complete dedication and purification before God? (vv. 23-24)

Biblical scholar Warren W. Wiersbe writes that this unique part of the ceremony symbolized that the priests "were set apart to **hear** God's voice, **do** God's work, and **walk** in God's ways". [1] Take a moment to touch or visualize each of these three extremities of yours as well, repeating this phrase as you do. Carry that visual with you as you go through your day.

7. FINAL CONSECRATION (Declaring Sacred) (vv. 30-36)

In biblical symbolism, seven is the number for completion. Where do we see this number in this last section, and what might be its meaning?

Now, let's talk about this in today's terms. What may seem like an irrelevant, old-fashioned ceremony becomes highly relevant when we read Peter's words in 1 Peter 2:5 and 2:9. Peter calls Christ-followers *"holy"* and *"a royal priesthood."*

Look back over the seven parts of the priesthood ceremony. How do these relate to your coming to Christ?

Weekend Reflection

WEEK 2

This week, we have taken a deeper look into the high priest, Aaron. The book of Leviticus repeatedly emphasizes the importance of the priesthood, especially the high priest. God entrusted the priests to carry out and enforce this entire book of laws. The elaborate ceremony we just studied in Leviticus 8 might lead us to believe that these priests, especially the high priest, should be extra good, righteous men, right?

However, Exodus 32 paints a very different picture. Shortly before the laws of Leviticus came to the people, the people had an idea. They were tired of waiting for Moses to come back with God's words, so they took matters into their own hands and decided to build a golden calf to worship instead. Any idea who took up the graving tool and fashioned this idol with his own two hands? It was a man named Aaron.

It appears Aaron could have spoken the same words about himself that the Apostle Paul spoke when he called himself *"the worst"* among sinners (1 Timothy 1:15, NIV). Yet God took an idol-carving, people-pleasing organizer and allowed him to be set apart as high priest, responsible for the moral direction of His nation. Just like God took Paul, a Christian-killing, angry, self-righteous Pharisee, and used him to preach the Good News of Jesus Christ to His world.

And, friend, if God can do that ... if He can take *"the worst"* of sinners and transform them into Kingdom warriors ... He can also use you and me (1 Timothy 1:15, NIV).

WEEK 3

DAY 11

Leviticus 9:1-24

THE GLORY OF THE LORD APPEARED AT THE INAUGURAL WORSHIP SERVICE.

Today's reading is about worship. In the previous chapters of Leviticus, God gave instructions; now it was time to start carrying those instructions out. And the very first worship service did not disappoint.

Before we dig into the text today, think of the most powerful worship service you have experienced. What do you remember about it? What made it special?

Leviticus 9:1 opens with the words, *"On the eighth day ..."* Let's take a moment to review.

Look back at Leviticus 8:35. What had been going on for the previous seven days?

For seven days, the priests were separated out. They literally lived outside the tent entrance and focused themselves solely on God. Biblical scholar Allan Moseley says, "Powerful public worship is so often preceded by powerful private worship." [1] What might this remind you of personally?

Finally the time came for Aaron to offer his first sacrifices. Everything was to be done exactly as the Lord commanded. Moses gave the instructions; then Aaron followed through.

Reading through Chapter 9, pay particular attention to the order of the animal sacrifices. Of the five offerings we have studied, which came first, both for Aaron himself and for the people of Israel? (vv. 8, 15)

Why do you think God commanded that this sacrifice be first?

Which of the five sacrifices came second, both for Aaron (v. 12) and the people? (v. 16)

Why might this be significant?

Finally, which sacrifice came last? (v. 18)

How does this follow the natural progression of our relationship with God?

Did you notice that Aaron first offered the sacrifices to address his own sin and commitment before he acted for the sins of the people?

Read Matthew 7:3–5. What similar sentiment does Jesus tell us?

This first worship service was so important. God used it to lay the foundation for how His people were to carry out His specific commands. It mattered that they followed God's instructions exactly. Rituals are just motions if there is no heart or follow-through.

Read Micah 6:6–8. How might the same principles apply to our worship today?

In Leviticus 9:6, Moses let the people know that this worship would usher in the glory of the Lord. And indeed it did.

According to verses 23-24, how did the glory of the Lord appear?

How did the people react?

The ESV uses the words *"shouted"* and *"fell on their faces"* (Leviticus 9:24). For some reason, I see those words and think it must have been in terror. However, the Hebrew word that is translated here as *"shouted"* is actually to exclaim with JOY! And *"fell on their faces"* doesn't mean they passed out. They were bowing in reverence and humility and awe.

Is your worship toward God characterized more by shouts of joy and celebration, or moments of reverence and awe? Why might we need both?

Biblical scholar John Hartley says, "The goal of worship in both testaments is to enter into God's presence." [2] Is this your goal in worship? Why or why not?

DAY 12

Leviticus 10:1-20

A DISRESPECTFUL ATTITUDE TOWARD GOD HAD SERIOUS CONSEQUENCES.

The worship service we studied yesterday was amazing. The glory of the Lord visibly came down as fire onto the altar. What a moment! The people shouted with joy and bowed in awe, which makes today's study feel like a sudden turn of events. And while this is a difficult story to read, it teaches us important lessons.

As we begin, go back and read Leviticus 8:4, 8:13 and 9:10. What common phrase do you see repeated?

Now notice what phrase ends Leviticus 10:1?

Let's try to understand what happened here. Nadab and Abihu attempted to burn incense, with fire from their own censers, before the Lord.

First we notice *"each took his censer and put fire in it"* (Leviticus 10:1). This was problem number one. The only censers that could be used were those that had been especially anointed with oil to mark them as holy. Also notice what word is used to describe Nadab and Abihu's fire in verse 1. Write it here:

According to Leviticus 16:12, the only fire allowed for burning incense before the Lord had to come from where? And according to Leviticus 9:24, who started that fire (the only authorized fire) on the altar?

Second problem: They attempted to burn incense before the Lord. Read Exodus 30:7. Who alone could place the incense before God?

The third problem we pick up from clues in Leviticus 16. Read Leviticus 16:1-2. After the mention of Aaron's sons dying, the Lord told Aaron not to enter where? We can assume that Nadab and Abihu must have made this attempt.

Interestingly, many scholars believe Leviticus 10:9 is another clue as to the serious disobedience shown by Aaron's sons. What does this verse specifically command for priests? What might that lead us to assume about these two men who died?

Based on all the clues gathered above, what does this lead you to believe about the attitude Nadab and Abihu had toward their duties and toward God?

Leviticus 10:4-7 can seem harsh. Aaron had just lost his two oldest sons. Eleazar and Ithamar had just lost their older brothers. And yet Moses tells them they cannot mourn their dead.

According to verse 7, why could they not go out and mourn (lest they die)?

I appreciate how Jay Sklar points out that God was not telling them they couldn't be sad, or to pretend like nothing happened.[1] Rather, it was a reminder to them of their holy assignment and calling. To leave and mourn the dead would have made them unclean. And at that present time, they were set apart for God's holy work. What similar lessons do we find in the New Testament from Jesus in Matthew 8:21-22 and Luke 14:25-26?

These are hard teachings. That's why it helps to consider the heart behind these teachings. What is God's heart here? What has priority in our life and why is this for our good?

After this dramatic display of punishment, it appears Aaron's next two sons made the next mistake.

According to Leviticus 10:16-17, why was Moses angry?

This time, Aaron jumped in to intervene. It is important to remember that priests could (and should) eat the sin sacrifice of the people. However, they could NOT eat a sin sacrifice that was offered on their own behalf. And after what had happened earlier to their brothers, the priests felt fully aware of their own personal sinful state. Therefore, in their hearts, they felt it wrong to eat the sin sacrifice this day. Now, let's make a few observations.

What was the difference between Nadab and Abihu's actions and Eleazar and Ithamar's?

Read 1 Samuel 16:7. How might this apply here as well?

DAY 13

Leviticus 11:1-47

THE DISTINCTION BETWEEN CLEAN AND UNCLEAN ANIMALS WAS A CONSTANT REMINDER OF HOLINESS TO GOD'S PEOPLE.

To begin today, let's start with a fun exercise. Below, you will find different kinds of foods. Beside each, put a check mark if the food is "good" and an X if the food is "bad" (in your own personal opinion).

CHOCOLATE CAKE		BROCCOLI	
SHRIMP AND GRITS		BACON	
TOMATO SOUP		CANDY CORN	
ICE CREAM		SPINACH	
TOFU		PICKLES	

Did you classify the foods as good or bad based on your own taste preferences? Did you classify them based on whether they were good or bad health-wise?

Jot down some ways that you (or others you know) have worshipped or honored God by what foods you did or did not eat. (For example, times of fasting; giving up particular foods in different seasons; or on the opposite end, eating a birthday cake for Jesus' birthday; or even times of celebrating the Lord's Supper.)

Today's lesson teaches us about the Lord's commands regarding clean (and edible) and unclean (and inedible) animals. Many theories have been suggested as to the Lord's classification. Some classify the animals for health reasons and the risks of some animals carrying disease. However, there are some holes in this theory (for example, undercooked pork can transfer disease, but then again, so can undercooked beef). Another theory suggests perhaps the Israelites associated the unclean animals with pagan religions surrounding them. Yet this doesn't seem to hold up either. (For example, a calf was considered "clean" in Israel yet was a prominent symbol in paganism.) Basically, we do not know exactly why some animals were clean and some were not. God does not give His reasoning, but we are given insight into His heart behind the laws. Let's break down the details of the animal classification to gain a better understanding of ancient Jewish life, and then let's look at three goals God established in this law.

The ancient world divided animals into three categories: land, water and sky.
In the chart below, read the verses in Leviticus 11 and provide a few examples of animals that were either edible or inedible. I added a few to get you started.

ANIMALS	LAND	WATER	SKY
CLEAN (edible)	vv. 2-3 Cows	v. 9 Trout	vv. 21-22 Crickets
UNCLEAN (inedible)	vv. 4-7, 29-30 Camels Mice	vv. 10-11 Shellfish	vv. 13-19, 20 Owls Bees

Starting in verse 24 of Leviticus 11, we learn that even touching the carcass of an unclean animal made a person (or whatever item that touched it) unclean. Notice this does not mean riding a camel made you unclean but rather touching a dead camel made you unclean. Also notice we are talking about "ritual purity" here. You could be ritually unclean, and this was not sin. You simply had to observe the rituals for becoming clean again. Does this sound like a lot of work? It was. It very much affected the Israelites' everyday life. And that was the point. Jay Sklar gives us three goals these rituals accomplished.[1]

1. IT SET GOD'S PEOPLE APART.

Fill in the words from Leviticus 11:45a:

"FOR I AM THE LORD WHO BROUGHT YOU UP ____________ _____

_____ ____________ OF EGYPT TO BE YOUR GOD."

What they did and did not eat distinguished the Israelites from the surrounding nations. They were **identified** by their food choices. According to John 13:35, what identifies Jesus-followers today?

2. IT REMINDED GOD'S PEOPLE OF GOD'S HOLINESS.

Fill in the words from Leviticus 11:45b.

"YOU SHALL THEREFORE BE HOLY, FOR _____ _______

_________________."

By accepting and obeying God's standards, the people exhibited their trust in God and that He knew best. Their obedience acknowledged that the Creator had a right to decide how to rule creation. It reminded them again their God was high and holy. What does Isaiah 55:8-9 teach us?

3. IT REMINDED GOD'S PEOPLE TO SEEK PURITY.

Fill in the words from Leviticus 11:45b.

"__________ SHALL THEREFORE ____ __________,

FOR I AM HOLY."

Every single meal they ate reminded them to stay pure. And moreover, if they were to put so much concern and care into food and ritual purity, then how much more so should they be concerned about moral purity? This was the point. To be clean outside was simply a reminder to be even more clean inside.

Keeping in mind all we have learned, read Jesus' words in Matthew 23:23-26. What are you reminded of in these words?

The new covenant we live under today, the beautiful blood Jesus shed on the cross, set aside these old-covenant, ritualistic cleanliness laws. Yet the heart behind the law remains ...

Read Mark 7:18-19. Jesus declared all food clean because it simply enters our stomachs, and we should be more concerned about our what?

Interesting Fact About Leviticus:

This might sound like a brain teaser, but it is a thought to keep in mind while reading Leviticus: What is holy is clean, but what is clean is not necessarily holy. What is unclean is common (ordinary, not holy) but not necessarily sinful. And that which is sinful is never clean and always ordinary (not holy).

DAY 14

Leviticus 12:1-8

WHILE CHILDBIRTH MADE A WOMAN UNCLEAN, GOD MADE A WAY FOR HER TO RETURN TO WORSHIP.

Recall the most recent baby-related news you have received. What did you feel? What were your first thoughts?

Let's establish, right from the start, God's heart toward children. What does Psalm 127:3 tell us?

In today's passage of Leviticus 12, we'll look at ancient purification rites after childbirth. While such a passage might not appear relevant to today's standards, remember we are looking behind these laws to show us God's heart, which is the same yesterday, today and always. And these laws actually show us a beautiful truth.

First, let's talk about why childbirth made a woman unclean. We established that children are, and were, a gift from God. Childbirth was a cause of great celebration in ancient Jewish culture as well. A baby did not make a woman unclean.

Rather, what made her unclean? (Leviticus 12:7)

Remember back to the first record of sin with Adam and Eve. With sin came curses. What was part of Eve's curse attached to, according to Genesis 3:16?

The next question some might ask is: "Why is a mother unclean for longer after giving birth to a female child?" Many theories have been presented here. Some see this and suggest it is sexist. However, this is inconsistent with what we know about God, which is that He created both male and female in His image. (Genesis 1:27) Some biblical scholars suggest it was medical. There is evidence that several ancient cultures believed the discharge after the birth of a female lasted longer than that of a male baby. [1] Other scholars suggest that perhaps because a female child also has the ability to bleed menstrually in the future, the mother took on the responsibility for her, too. [2] Still another possibility is that, because the baby boy was to be brought to the tabernacle for his circumcision ceremony on the eighth day, the shortened time for baby boys allowed the mother to attend. [3] Honestly, we do not know exactly why. So let's look at what we do know ...

In Leviticus 12:6, it says,

"AND WHEN THE DAYS OF HER PURIFYING ARE COMPLETED, WHETHER FOR A SON OR FOR A DAUGHTER, ________ ________ ____________ TO THE PRIEST AT THE ENTRANCE OF THE TENT OF MEETING A LAMB A YEAR OLD FOR A BURNT OFFERING, AND A PIGEON OR A TURTLEDOVE FOR A SIN OFFERING ..."

Just to be clear, who brought the sacrifice? In other words, who was allowed to come and worship before God?

This is the heart of God. It is to provide a way for everyone He loves and created to come before Him, to worship Him. God will always be there for us. He sent Jesus to erase sin and the pain of the curse that it brought, and to make a way for us to be with Him forever.

In light of today's reading, take a moment and read Revelation 22:1-5. What is the heart of God and the future for both man- and woman-kind?

DAY 15

Leviticus 13:1-59

THOSE WITH UNCLEAN SKIN AFFLICTIONS LIVED OUTSIDE THE CAMP TO PRESERVE THE HEALTH OF THE WHOLE.

The year 2020 — is it too soon to process yet? To get us into a proper frame of mind for today's passage, let's take a moment to reflect on how life changed as a result of the COVID-19 pandemic.

Where were you when you first heard the term "COVID-19"? Many activities, gatherings and places were shut down. People were asked to stay home. So many have tragically lost their lives. What words would you use to describe that time?

Some have stayed home because they felt forced to or maybe because they were afraid of getting sick themselves. Others have felt a real fear for the safety of their loved ones around them. Whatever thoughts you have toward the year 2020, I think we can understand Leviticus 13 better in light of our experience.

What is the heading for Leviticus 13 in your Bible?

Traditionally, the Hebrew term *ṣāra'at* used in Leviticus 13 has been translated as "leprosy." Nearly all scholars agree that this is not a good translation. Today when we hear the word "leprosy," we think of the condition known as Hansen's disease, a disease that appears on the skin and results in loss of nerve feelings and even the falling off of the coldest extremities. This is not what appears to be addressed in Leviticus 13. In fact, many scholars say there is no evidence of this type of "leprosy" in the ancient Near East at this time. [1] So instead, throughout this chapter, we are talking about other various types of defiling skin diseases.

Verses 1-44 explain in great detail how a priest was to diagnose *ṣāra'at*. Verses 45-46 then hand out the consequences of being declared unclean. We find two paths. Either the priest instantly declared a person unclean and moved straight to the consequences, or ...

What would have happened if the diagnosis wasn't obviously "unclean"? (vv. 4-5, 21, 26-27, 31-32)

Let's look now at the consequences of being declared unclean because of a defiling skin disease.

According to verses 45-46, an unclean person:

Had to wear ______________ clothes, let their hair ____________ , and cover their ______________ .

(These were all ancient signs of mourning.)

Had to cry out "___________ , ________________" (a warning to others).

Had to live where?

The rest of Leviticus 13 talks about *"a case of leprous disease in a garment"* (v. 47). We will later see that this could also apply to a house, probably due to mold, mildew or other fungal infestations.

What might happen to a home, garment, etc. if mold and mildew were left untreated?

Today we have the God-given blessings of scientists and doctors who have taught us much about disease, viruses, bacteria, fungus, etc. Yet if the COVID-19 pandemic has taught us anything, it is that all of our knowledge still does not mean we have control over what these things can do. In ancient times, the law required people with defiling skin diseases to live outside the camp for the health of the whole. It also served as a reminder that disease had no business in the presence of God. Read that again. And don't misunderstand. This is not saying that God is disgusted with us when we are ill. Not at all! Simply look at Jesus, who, instead of running away from a man with true leprosy, reached out and touched him! (Matthew 8:3) God draws us close in sickness. But He wants us to know that He hates disease! And don't you, too?! Disease has no place in the presence of God, and we can see this as the reassurance that heaven will have no disease. It won't be allowed there!

Take a moment to think about how our lives are connected. What one person does will affect others. In what ways is your life affecting those around you and vice versa?

Read Revelation 21:4. What does it remind you about heaven?

Finally, I cannot help but think of the people throughout history who had to live in isolation for the protection of the community. Who can you think of who is maybe living an isolated life? How can you pray for them today?

Weekend Reflection

WEEK 3

For Week 3, let's look deeper into purification rites after childbirth, specifically looking at Leviticus 12:6-8. After a woman completed the first two steps, one final purification step remained. The law required her to bring a year-old lamb to the temple for a burnt offering, and a pigeon or dove for a sin offering. At that point, the law declared her thoroughly and completely clean.

God did provide for one exception. If the new mother could not afford a lamb, she could instead offer two pigeons or doves for her burnt and sin offerings. All along the way, the Lord has provided ways for those sitting at the poverty line, struggling under financial strains where the bills are more than the change in their pockets. It's clear the Lord desires all people to come and worship. Not just the wealthy, put-together men and women. No, God longs for all of His people to come to Him.

And nowhere does He showcase this exception better than in Luke 2:24. On that day, a young, unmarried woman who had given birth to a baby boy observed the purification laws and came to offer her sacrifice. Luke tells us that this young woman named Mary, with a swaddled-up baby Jesus in her arms, brought two birds. Birds — because she couldn't afford a lamb.

And just as God provided a way for this new mother to come before Him in worship to her God who had given her such an amazing gift, He also used that gift to provide *every single one of us* a way to worship Him as well. Because of Jesus Christ, God has made provisions so that every man and woman, young, old, rich, poor, with every color of skin and speaking every language, has an opportunity to worship the Lord God! Jesus paid the price we could not afford. He cleansed us completely, and He welcomes us into the throne room of God.

WEEK 4

DAY 16

Leviticus 14:1-57

GOD PROVIDED A WAY FOR THE UNCLEAN TO BE DECLARED CLEAN AGAIN.

In Chapter 13, we talked about *ṣāraʿat*, the Hebrew word for defiling diseases that our English Bibles sometimes translate as "leprosy." However, we learned that leprosy, as we know it, isn't perhaps the best definition. Chapter 13 talked about what to look for in disease and when to declare a person (or garment) unclean. Being declared unclean held consequences to protect the community, the hardest of which was isolation from camp. I am so thankful that Leviticus doesn't stop this discussion in Chapter 13. Because in today's reading of Chapter 14 we see God make a way for a person to be declared clean. This is the heart of God. God longs to declare His people clean and to gather them together in His arms!

Leviticus 14 addresses ritual cleansing for ritual impurities. And though Jesus' coming made these rituals obsolete, it did not make them irrelevant! In fact, in these ritual cleansings we often find hints and reminders for our own moral cleansing. Let me show you how ...

THE PRIEST

Read Leviticus 14:1-3, and pay particular attention to the priest. Where does he go? From what we've learned so far, where would the priest usually be found?

Let's look at this for its symbolism. In a similar way, Jesus left where, according to John 6:38?

And Jesus did so to do what, according to Luke 19:10?

TWO BIRDS

In Leviticus 14:4–7, the cleansing process involved two birds. The first bird was killed over what? (v. 5)

What is *"mortal flesh"* (2 Corinthians 4:11) referred to as in 2 Corinthians 4:7?

Back to Leviticus 14:6–7: What was done to the second bird?

Let's look at the symbolism found here. The priest killed one bird over a clay jar and sprinkled its blood over a living bird, which flew up and carried the impurity away with it. How does this remind you of Jesus? (1 Corinthians 15:3–4)

WASHING

To set the scene clearly, let's return to Leviticus 14:7. Fill in the blank:

"AND HE SHALL SPRINKLE IT SEVEN TIMES ON HIM WHO IS TO BE CLEANSED OF THE LEPROUS DISEASE. THEN HE SHALL ____________ ______ ____________ AND SHALL LET THE LIVING BIRD GO INTO THE OPEN FIELD."

In Leviticus 14:8-9, what did a person do after the priest declared them clean?

In a similar way, Jesus heals our sin. He declares us "clean." Receiving that declaration of salvation produces so much joy! It will also compel us to want to do something else. What is that, according to 2 Corinthians 7:1?

Not only do we want to wash up, but we will also want new "clothes." What do we now put on, according to Colossians 3:12-14?

Did you notice the emphasis on shaving all the hair? Not only was this sanitary, but it showed the skin to be clear and smooth, like a baby's. It symbolized a "rebirth." What does Jesus say in John 3:3?

SACRIFICES

On the eighth day, the priests offered sacrifices to complete the cleansing ritual. Yet notice something unique about this passage. According to Leviticus 14:14, what did the priest do with some of the blood?

Who also did a similar ritual in Leviticus 8:24 and to whom did he do it?

Our gracious and good God takes us, defiled, outcast and unclean, and He treats us like priests. Take a moment and write what that means to you.

HOUSES

Starting in Leviticus 14:33, the rest of the chapter is dedicated to the cleansing of houses. We mentioned earlier that this was probably dealing with mold, mildew and other fungi. Such infestations spread quickly and could cause major destruction as well as disease. According to verse 45, what would they do to a house that could not be cleaned?

Is there any "unclean stone" that you need to remove from your home or life before its uncleanness begins to spread? How is this similar to Jesus' words of hyperbole in Matthew 5:29-30?

DAY 17

Leviticus 15:1-33

GOD'S LAWS ON BODILY DISCHARGE TAUGHT ABOUT SEX.

When I was in the fifth grade, our school held a "program." One day, all the fifth-grade boys left to watch a film. They returned, some avoiding eye contact, some nudging each other with grins. I had no idea what was going on ... until the next day when all the girls were called to the assembly. We watched a film talking about monthly cycles. I'm pretty sure the mom in the film made a uterus shape out of pancake batter. We left with feminine products in hand, and faces red in embarrassment. Maybe you, too, get a similar awkward feeling when reading Leviticus 15. While you and I might feel uncomfortable, I am also so thankful that God doesn't shy away from talking about our bodies. And it's so interesting what His purity laws here have to teach us about sex.

In this chapter, you'll see the term "discharge" and the phrase "his/her body" often. The term "discharge" in Hebrew, *zwb*, means "flowing," as in fluid. The phrase "his/her body" in Hebrew, *bāśār*, is actually a euphemism for genitals. With that established, let's notice how this chapter is set up. It is what we call an "AB-BA" pattern.

A - (v. 3) An abnormal case of male discharge.
B - (v. 16) A normal case of male emission of semen.
B - (v. 19) A normal case of female menstrual impurity.
A - (v. 25) An abnormal case of female discharge of blood.

Now before we go any further, let's establish God's attitude toward sex right from the beginning of time.

What did God say in Genesis 1:28? How about Genesis 2:24?

God created sex. He designed it. And sex, in His design, is not sin. Therefore, remember, as we study this chapter, becoming "unclean" was not a sin! So what was the purpose of these laws? That's what we want to dig into because when we find the purpose and heart behind the laws we see what they have to teach us today.

HYGIENE

One obvious conclusion is that these laws dealt with hygiene. Some scholars suggest the abnormal male discharge refers to gonorrhea, a sexually transmitted disease. Today we know of many diseases spread through the exchange of fluids during sex. Also, as any woman can tell you, personal hygiene, especially during the monthly cycle, is so important.

Why do you think God might be concerned with our personal hygiene? What does this tell you about God's care for you?

SEPARATION FROM PAGAN PRACTICES

While hygiene is important, I want to suggest that this is maybe not the main purpose of these laws. There is something more going on here. Specifically, God set forth many of the purity laws we have been studying (what foods to eat, how and when to wash, etc.) to separate the Jewish people from their gentile neighbors. It marked them as different. It showed that they trusted the one true Creator and followed His rules for them. This included the laws on bodily discharges. Surrounding pagan religions used sexual activity to worship their gods. They believed having sex with the temple prostitutes encouraged the gods to "fertilize the soil with rain." [1] There were numerous "fertilization rites" a person could perform to the gods. And many of these practices were done in the pagan god's shrine ...

With this in mind, while sex in the right context is not a sin, for ancient Jews the discharge from sex caused a person to become what? (Leviticus 15:18)

And anything declared unclean could not be in God's temple. (Leviticus 15:31) Therefore, distinctly **unlike** the surrounding nations, God did not want what happening inside His temple?

This leads us to our next point ...

SEX IS NOT GOD

In this time period, sex was a big focus. Not only did people enjoy it, but they actually had a great desire to have big families with many children. These purity rules regulated sex for them. They had to think about whether or not it was a good time to be "unclean" for the day. Women had a monthly seven-day period (no pun intended) where both the husband's and wife's focus would be on something other than sex. As the *New American Commentary* on Leviticus points out, these rules were "one way of indicating that sexual involvement should not be an obsession in life." [2] They needed to know, as perhaps we do today, that sex isn't God.

From top-rated movies to bestselling books, advertisements and internet websites, how would you say our society today views sex?

In what ways are we, as Christ-followers, called to be different from our culture in regard to sex?

ESPECIALLY HARD (BUT HOLY) SECTIONS

MENSTRUATION:
WHAT DID IT MEAN TO BE "UNCLEAN"?

As a woman, there is a good chance you read through Leviticus 15:19-24 and at least raised an eyebrow. It is estimated that a woman will experience 400-500 periods during her lifetime. Menstrual cycles shape a woman's life, from puberty to menopause. And yet they can often feel like a source of shame or embarrassment. Many in the world place the blame for "period shame" on religion, and particularly on verses like we have read in Leviticus. Are there grounds for these thoughts? What was God's intent in declaring women "unclean" approximately 60 days a year from around the age of 12 until somewhere around 51? And really, what's the deal with periods? Let's take a look ...

First and foremost, let's establish that God created the bodies of both men and women. He created them specifically, on purpose. And Romans 1:20 tells us that it is through God's creation that He reveals qualities of Himself. Which means, yes, God designed and created even menstrual cycles to teach us. Have you ever studied the science behind ovulation and menstruation? There is an orchestra of movements happening, a delicate dance of hormones taking place, that is truly remarkable and honestly mind-blowing. Maybe you are thinking, *How can something so beautiful sometimes be so painful ... and messy?*

Let's talk about this word "unclean" in Leviticus. The Hebrew word here, *ṭā·mē*, meant a state of ritual impurity. It was not a statement on hygiene. It didn't mean "dirty" or "gross" at all! And it also did not mean "sinful." So why did a period result in becoming ritually "unclean"? It all comes down to one thing: blood.

Leviticus 17:11 is a key verse not just for Leviticus and Old Testament sacrifices, and not even just because it explains the importance of Jesus' sacrifice (although this is a big one!). It also explains something about periods. Leviticus 17:11 says, *"For the life of the flesh is in the blood, and I have given it to you on the altar to make atonement for your souls ..."* God set blood apart because blood represented life. And isn't it interesting that the part of a woman that has the potential to bring forth new life ends each cycle of possibility with blood? That blood washes away the old lining to make way for the new. It seems like a familiar picture, doesn't it? Blood washing away the old, dead ways to make a way to new life? And every month, a woman's body bears witness to this reminder again.

So, yes, the Old Testament set blood apart as a visual reminder. And, yes, because of this, God declared women ritually unclean for seven days each cycle. Not dirty or gross or sinful. Just separated for a moment to remind us of the price of bringing new life.

But what about today? What about New Testament living? Well, today we have Jesus. And Jesus' blood and sacrifice washed away the old ways of sin and death (1 John 1:7) and gave us birth to new life in Him! (2 Corinthians 5:17) He is the fulfillment! (Matthew 5:17) Therefore, we no longer need ritual cleanliness laws. And Jesus then gave a new commission: *"Go therefore and make disciples of all nations, baptizing them in the name of the Father and of the Son and of the Holy Spirit, teaching them to observe all that I have commanded you"* (Matthew 28:19-20a). As Rachel Jones puts it in her book *A Brief Theology of Periods*, "So for God's people today, this is the main way we bring life into the world: not by bearing children but by making disciples. Or rather, the call to bear children is part of a bigger mission; we are to model and teach the gospel to any children we are blessed with ..." [1] Our new purpose is to bring forth life in Christ's Church.

Turns out, there is a lot my period can tell me. Feeling shame isn't from God! God created our bodies in an amazing and profound way, and as fellow bearers of life, women get a unique view into the cost of both sin and life. We bear the reminder monthly. But, praise Jesus, He is the fulfiller of all God's promises! His blood sets us free. And He calls us to join Him in bringing new life. Perhaps there is a lot I can reflect on the next time my monthly visitor stops by.

IF YOU'D LIKE TO READ MORE ABOUT THIS TOPIC, SEE OUR ENDNOTES SECTION ON PAGE 208 FOR A LIST OF RECOMMENDED RESOURCES.

DAY 18

Leviticus 16:1-34

THE DAY OF ATONEMENT WAS THE ONLY TIME THE HIGH PRIEST COULD ENTER THE HOLY PLACE AND MAKE FULL ATONEMENT.

To prepare our minds and hearts for today, let's begin with a quick exercise.

Try to think of every sin you have ever committed. Do you think it would be possible to list every single one? Why or why not?

Today we'll focus on the Day of Atonement. Yes, this day was an important day for ancient Judaism. But it is also immensely important for us to understand as well.

Let's go back and look again at the daily sin sacrifices offered in Leviticus 4. According to Leviticus 4:1, these were for anyone who sinned how?

The daily sin sacrifices we have looked at covered mistakes. But what about unintentional sin? God addresses that here. Once the people became aware of their guilt, they could seek forgiveness.

However, this really begs two questions. First, what if they did not become aware of their sin? And second, what if their sin was intentional or deliberate?

Both then and now, because God is completely holy, there can be absolutely no sin before Him. Not the really big ones, and not even the ones we didn't realize we had done. But in His love and compassion, God made a way for His people to still be in a relationship with Him and to cover the sin that separated them from Him. In the Old Testament this was called the Day of Atonement. However, the Day of Atonement was only meant to be a foreshadowing of what we have today. And for us, it (or rather He) is called Jesus. Let's take a look ...

In Leviticus 16:2a there is a reference to *"the Holy Place inside the veil."* The original language makes this seem somewhat confusing, but when we apply what we know about the tabernacle and connect it to verses like Hebrews 9:3, we can see that this was a reference to a very specific area within the Holy Place, called the Most Holy Place. The Holy Place held the lampstand, the table for the bread, and the altar of incense. At the back of the Holy Place, behind a veil, was the Most Holy Place. Inside the Most Holy Place was the Ark of the Covenant, which had the mercy seat on top, which was the throne of God. This is where God's presence resided on earth.

Not just anyone could enter into God's presence either. Leviticus 16 starts out referencing Aaron's two sons. What happened to them?

What would happen to Aaron or any high priest who tried to enter the Most Holy Place uninvited? (v. 2)

According to verses 3 and 29, the high priest could only enter the Most Holy Place when? (For our modern-day calendars, this was during the harvest, sometime in September or October.)

Interesting Fact About Leviticus:

Chiastic structure was commonly used among Hebrew texts. Chiastic structure is a way of presenting information in the form of a pattern. It typically starts with information A, then goes to information B, with information C right in the middle. Next comes a look again at information B, and ending with another look at information A (in total: ABCBA). In chiastic structure, information C is seen as the main focus of what is shared. Interestingly, if we look at the Torah (Genesis, Exodus, Leviticus, Numbers, Deuteronomy) as chiastic, Leviticus would be the most important. If we were to break down the book of Leviticus into chiastic structure, the most important part would be the Day of Atonement.

Read Hebrews 9:24. Where did Jesus enter? Why is this like the Most Holy Place, only better?

In Leviticus 16:11, the high priest **first** had to offer a sin offering for what? Why might this be important?

Read Hebrews 7:26-28. What is different about Jesus?

We established that the high priest entered the Most Holy Place once a year, every year. Read Hebrews 9:25-26. How is Jesus' sacrifice different?

According to Leviticus 16:14-16, what was offered to make atonement?

According to Hebrews 9:25-26, what did Jesus offer?

Friends, Jesus is our Day of Atonement every single day we profess to be followers of Him. He covers all of our sins, big and small, intentional and unknown. He is the perfect sacrifice, covering all of our guilt and shame and allowing us to stand before a holy God.

Pause and think about the system established in Leviticus 16 and the Day of Atonement. Then slowly and carefully read through Hebrews 9:11-15. On the following page, write down your thoughts.

Interesting Fact About Leviticus:

The Hebrew word *ăzā'zēl* is presented in the ESV as *"Azazel"* and in the NIV as *"the scapegoat."* Biblical scholar Mark Rooker says there are four different explanations proposed as to the interpretation of this word. [1]

#1. The word *ăzā'zēl* describes the goat's function. Combine the root *'zl*, meaning "go away," and *'z*, meaning "goat," and you have "the goat that goes away." This is how it received the English translation of "scapegoat."

#2. The word *ăzā'zēl* is an abstract noun meaning "entire removal" and therefore describes the theological concept that the goat is a picture of sin being removed.

#3. The word *ăzā'zēl* is a reference to a location. This comes from the thought that the root, *'zz*, means "strong, fierce," which probably depicts the terrain of the goat's destination.

#4. In the intertestamental work of *1 Enoch*, there is a reference to a demon named *ăzā'zēl*, leading some to think this was a reference to a demon in the wilderness.

DAY 19

Leviticus 17:1-9

SACRIFICES COULD ONLY BE MADE BEFORE THE TABERNACLE.

When each of my daughters received her first cell phone, it came with a parent contract that gave us the right to take and scan their phone anytime, anywhere. We explained to them the idea of accountability and how it helps us think more about what we are saying or doing if we know someone is checking in. You might say a similar situation took place in Leviticus 17:1–9.

In Leviticus 17, God outlines where animals may be killed and sacrifices offered.

Where is this place, according to verse 4?

To help us understand, let's look at the context. What can we assume was happening according to verse 7?

Today, let's learn a new word: **syncretism**. Syncretism is the attempt to blend together two different, sometimes even opposing, ideas or doctrines. It might be difficult for us to imagine worshiping both the One True God and a "goat demon" at the same time. Yet as Jay Sklar points out, "Polytheism was to ancient Israel what materialism is to many today: it was so much a part of the cultural air they breathed that they were very slow to turn from it, even after deciding to follow the Lord." [1]

What worldly ideas try to blend together with Christianity? Why might it be tempting to blend two different doctrines together?

God limited the killing of animals for sacrifice to the front of the tabernacle. This kept people honest. If someone saw their neighbor killing an animal outside the camp, the neighbor couldn't pretend like they were offering it to the Lord. There is only One True God, and He expected His people to worship only the One who is real. God was demanding exclusivity. They couldn't pretend to love God, but also love false gods.

What does Leviticus 17:7 compare such worshippers to?

What did Joshua tell the people later on, in Joshua 24:15?

What does Jesus say in Matthew 6:24?

While nearly all scholars agree this is the primary purpose of the laws in Leviticus 17:1-9, several scholars also offer a secondary observation. They believe that the text refers not only to animals killed for sacrifice but also to any animal killed for food. Some even suggest that, because meat was too costly during this time, perhaps the only time people killed their animals to eat would have been for the fellowship offering. In either case, slaying any animal could only take place before the tabernacle. According to biblical scholar Warren Wiersbe, "By this law the Lord dignified ordinary meals and made them a sacred experience."[2] When meat is consumed, it is a matter of one creature giving its life for the life of another. It is, in effect, a type of sacrifice.

According to Leviticus 17:4, what would have been imputed to the man who killed an animal somewhere other than before the tabernacle and before the Lord? (This word essentially means "murder.")

"To treat creation with respect is to respect the Creator." Do you agree or disagree with this statement? Why?

What is one way today that you can show respect to God for the blessings He has given you?

DAY 20

Leviticus 17:10-16

BLOOD REPRESENTS LIFE.

I sometimes wonder what non-Christians think when they hear the songs we sing and the way we talk about Jesus' blood. To an outsider, it might appear like we have a gruesome fascination.

Write down familiar worship song lyrics that mention blood.

Why, as modern-day Christians, are we so interested in Jesus' blood? The answer starts way back here, in Leviticus 17. Leviticus 17:10 set a law that prohibited eating blood (either directly or by consuming raw meat). The purpose of this law was very clear. Blood was to be respected. Every time His people saw blood, God desired it to trigger a thought in their minds. Let's take a deeper look.

According to Leviticus 17:11, what was *"in the blood"*?

This is huge. Let's not rush past this. If we were to make it into a simple equation, we could say

"BLOOD = ______________ ."

Verse 11 goes on to say who has *"given it for you"*?

Let's stop again. That word *"I"* means "I, myself." There is an emphasis on it. God is saying all life belongs to Him. All life is from God, created by God. This means, as followers of God, we should care for and respect life in all its forms, from humans to animals to plants. What is one way today that you can show respect to God by caring for the life He has created?

Verse 11 tells us what the blood can do. It says, *"... and I have given it for you on the altar to make"* what?

Let's finish verse 11. The blood makes atonement by what?

Here's the truth: We are sinners. Sin is ugly and messy and mean. Every single one of us deserves the price of sin, which is death. Yet God, in His love and mercy, wanted to make a way for us to escape the punishment of sin. It would still cost a life. That life in the Old Testament was an innocent animal's. It wasn't perfect, but it taught God's people that sin was costly. It cost someone, or in this case, something, their life. God's plan, before time began, was for that blood to someday point to the innocent One who would hang on a cross, spill His blood, give His life, so that you and I could have life instead. Just look at what the blood of Jesus has accomplished ...

ROMANS 5:9 — By His blood, we are ______________________.

EPHESIANS 1:7 — Through His blood, we have ______________.

REVELATION 1:5 — By His blood, He has __________________________.

EPHESIANS 2:13 — By His blood, we have been ______________________________ .

1 JOHN 1:7 — His blood ______________________________ .

ACTS 20:28 — With His own blood, He ______________________________ .

Write one sentence about what the blood of Jesus means to you.

Weekend Reflection

WEEK 4

Let's take a deeper look into this idea of being unclean. This week we have studied laws for cleansing lepers, and laws about bodily discharges. Sometimes in reading these, we can separate ourselves from what these laws really meant for real-life people. I think that's why I love that Mark took the time to address both of these issues in his Gospel account of Jesus.

In Mark 1:40, a leper went to Jesus. From what we have learned, we know that this man had to live outside town, socially isolated from others. He had to walk around shouting that he was unclean. People would have run at the sound of his voice. They would have crossed to the other side of the road to avoid coming close. He wasn't allowed inside the town, much less anywhere near the temple of God.

And yet this Jesus he had heard about just so happened to be walking outside town, close enough that the leprous man could try to come toward Him. Do you think the man was shocked when Jesus didn't run away? And not only that! We know that Jesus had the power to heal just from saying the words, and yet … Jesus intentionally reached out and touched him. When was the last time this man had felt the warmth of human touch? Maybe that touch healed not only the man's leprosy but also his wounded heart.

Later, in Mark 5:25, we learn of another encounter with Jesus. This time we meet a woman who had been bleeding for 12 years. From what we have learned in Leviticus, we know that a discharge like this made this woman unclean. What is difficult to imagine, on top of the physical discomfort and concern, is what it must have felt like to be unclean for 12 straight years. Anyone who touched you or your bed or your chair was unclean for the day and had to undergo rigorous washing. Do you imagine people stopping their visits? Maybe they took a step back so as not to even accidentally brush up against her. I wonder if she felt like a burden to her family and friends. And yet here comes Jesus, who can take it all away. And she dared not approach Him outright, but maybe if she could secretly touch His garment, then He wouldn't know that she had made Him unclean for the day. But Jesus wasn't about to let her hide in shame. He called her out, and Scripture says she confessed in *"fear and trembling"* (Mark 5:33). Then she waited for His wrath. But instead, she heard His warm voice say, *"Daughter, your faith has made you well"* (Mark 5:34).

We, too, may read Leviticus at times and wonder to ourselves, *Is God good?* His holiness is so big, it sometimes feels scary. But the minute our minds wander that road, we stop and remember how Jesus made time for and loved broken, outcast, hurting, unclean people. This is the heart of God. Love and mercy and, yes, His holiness, too — all of it is what makes our God good.

WEEK 5

DAY 21

Leviticus 18:1-30

GOD MADE RULES FOR HIS CREATION REGARDING SEXUAL RELATIONS.

As a parent, I have established rules for my children. Some I chose for their health, like how much sugar to eat and going to bed at a certain hour. These are good rules that have a little flexibility. There are other rules, however, that are absolutes. For example, we don't drink the cleaner under the sink, and we always wear our seat belts in the car. The consequences for breaking these rules could be dire.

Until now, we've studied what scholars refer to as "ritual" laws. These are laws that set God's people apart and taught them to respect God and His tabernacle. After establishing these laws, Leviticus moved on to what scholars call "moral" laws. Disobeying the moral law violated God's plan and purpose and therefore His omnipotence. And as we will later learn in Chapter 20, this disobedience had serious consequences.

Let's start in Leviticus 18:1-5.

Underline every time you see the phrase *"I am the Lord..."* How many times do you find it?

Two of those instances add *"I am the Lord* ***your God****"* (emphasis added). To worship Jesus as Lord and Savior means trusting His love and His sovereignty, and following Him and His ways instead of our own.

Likewise, Leviticus 18:1-5 says twice that His people were to keep what?

There is a saying that goes: "With great privilege comes great responsibility." Whether you believe this quote came from Voltaire, Winston Churchill or the great Spiderman, the premise behind it is true. Jesus said, *"From everyone who has been given much, much will be demanded"* (Luke 12:48b, NIV). Israel had the great privilege of being God's special people through whom He would bless the world. But with this title came the great responsibility of living as God required.

Read 1 Peter 2:9. What great privileges have Christ-followers been given and what kinds of responsibilities might these invoke? How might this quote also apply to your life as a follower of Jesus?

To love God is to follow and respect the laws He designed for His creation. And part of His creation includes sexual beings. As Jay Sklar says, "Human sexuality is a good part of the Lord's creation, but in a sinful world, it can be misused." [1] Let's take a look ...

In the ESV, the term used in Leviticus 18:6-18 is *"uncover the nakedness."* This is an idiom for sexual relations, specifically in a negative or illicit way. What "category" of people did this law prohibit from having sexual relations together?

We understand the dangers of incest, but notice this list exceeds beyond just blood relatives. This prohibited sexual relations with any relative, even by law or by marriage. Yes, this law protected the integrity of women especially, but it also protected men. Home was to be a safe place. Why do you think this was important?

If you or someone you know has been the victim of sexual abuse, whether by a family member, family "friend" or anyone else, please know God knows, sees and feels your pain. He sees you and loves you. Psalm 56:8 says, *"You have kept count of my tossings; put my tears in your bottle. Are they not in your book?"* Let's take a quiet moment to pray for the Lord's love and healing to touch any heart that has been hurt by the sin of sexual abuse.

Verses 19-23 provide other sexual regulations. Write them here. (Side note: Having sex during menstruation is the only prohibited act from this passage that is not mentioned anywhere in the New Testament.)

Verses 24-30 use a vivid analogy to describe what the land will do when it becomes unclean. What do these scriptures say?

Finally, what are the last six words of this chapter? Write them below.

We've covered some sensitive topics. But at the heart of it all, we find a good and loving God who asks us to trust Him. His ways sometimes differ from the ways of the world and surrounding culture, just like He asked Israel to be different from Egypt and Canaan. How can you show God that He alone is the Lord your God, and you will follow His ways today?

ESPECIALLY HARD (BUT HOLY) SECTIONS

HOMOSEXUALITY

While there are only two verses within Leviticus dealing with homosexuality (Leviticus 18:22 and 20:13), it is indeed a hot-button topic today that brings many emotions and questions. Let's see if we can prayerfully address some of these questions.

IS HOMOSEXUALITY WRONG?

Some Christians today contend there is nothing wrong with a faithful and loving homosexual marriage/relationship. However, this position seems inconsistent when we read the Bible as a whole. The Old Testament as well as the New Testament call homosexuality a sin (in the New Testament, see, for example, 1 Corinithians 6:9, Romans 1:27 and 1 Timothy 1:8-11). Additionally, when Jesus and His apostles warn against *"sexual immorality,"* a phrase used 23 times throughout the New Testament, what they had in mind was, without question, anything sexual outside of a marriage between a man and woman. Let's try our best to understand their words today and how they would intend us to hear them.

IF WE CHOSE TO OBEY THE LEVITICAL LAWS ABOUT HOMOSEXUALITY, SHOULDN'T WE OBEY ALL LEVITICAL LAWS?

Let's revisit the three categories of Levitical law. Some were ceremonial. These laws addressed sacrifices, clean and unclean food, washings, etc. Jesus completely fulfilled the ceremonial laws. Therefore, they no longer apply today. Other Levitical laws were civil laws given specifically for the nation's judicial system. These laws provided order and issued punishments for disobedience. Because these laws were specific to the nation of Israel during this time, we don't follow the same use of punishment. The final category of laws concerned morality. The moral law distinguishes right from wrong, like honesty and generosity from lying or stealing. These are laws that never change and always apply. Within the context of Leviticus, rules regarding sexual sin fall within the moral law and are meant to be followed today.

IS GOD BEING UNFAIR?

As Creator, God has the right and authority to govern how we are to "use" the creation He has made. We acknowledge that we report to a Higher Being who knows and loves us. When we say "yes" to Jesus, we surrender to Him. We make Him Lord of our lives. He is God. Sex is not. And sexual orientation is not the "essence" of a person. We are created for more than sex and sexual fulfillment. Counter to what culture wants to tell us, sex is not everything.

ARE CHRISTIANS JUDGMENTAL?

Here is a question for the heart. Studies show gay youth in particular experience hatred from others, are guilt-ridden and commit suicide in high numbers. Those looking to understand these tragic losses of life sometimes turn and point to the Bible. And while it is true that some Christians have engaged in both abusive behavior and language toward those who are gay or who otherwise do not agree with biblical paradigms of gender and sexuality, this is not acceptable and is NOT Christ-like behavior. As the Church, God calls us to reach out and help the broken, lost and hurting because He created and values all human life. The Church ... we ... are His hands and feet on this earth to love and care for everyone, even those we may disagree with. Jesus set this example so beautifully. Love leads with both truth and grace. Someone once said homosexuality seems to be the one sin the Church expects a person to clean up before they enter the Church. But, in reality, the Church is a hospital! That's the only reason you and I can be there, too. God created the Church for hurting, broken and sinful people like us to come to Jesus and find salvation, healing and hope. And then take what we've found and share it with whoever and wherever God takes us. And while we should never compromise God's Word, we are called to come alongside and love those who struggle with sin. We are to treat everyone with understanding, kindness and grace.

WHAT SHOULD I DO IF A FRIEND OR FAMILY MEMBER COMES OUT TO ME?

I found Sam Allberry's steps, from his book *Is God Anti-Gay?*, incredibly helpful and encouraging. [1] He says first, thank the family member or friend for being open. It is a privilege to be trusted and told something so personal. Next, assure them that they do not need to fear your rejection. You still love and value your relationship with them. If they specifically ask for your thoughts, he advises you to explain that Christians have a different view on matters of sexuality than culture does, and that you would be happy to talk about that another time. But now, you really want to listen and hear their heart. Then, listen. Really listen. Ask questions. How did they come to this realization? How have they been treated? This not only gives you empathy but also builds the relationship. Finally, offer to pray for them and ask how they would like you to pray. And then do just that. Pray. Pray and trust Jesus, who loves them deeply.

IF YOU'D LIKE TO READ MORE ABOUT THIS TOPIC, SEE OUR ENDNOTES SECTION ON PAGE 208 FOR A LIST OF RECOMMENDED RESOURCES.

THE TEN COMMANDMENTS

EXODUS 20:1-17

And God spoke all these words, saying,

I. I am the LORD your God, who brought you out of the land of Egypt, out of the house of slavery. You shall have no other gods before me.

II. You shall not make for yourself a carved image, or any likeness of anything that is in heaven above, or that is in the earth beneath, or that is in the water under the earth. You shall not bow down to them or serve them ...

III. You shall not take the name of the LORD your God in vain ...

IV. Remember the Sabbath day, to keep it holy ...

V. Honor your father and your mother ...

VI. You shall not murder.

VII. You shall not commit adultery.

VIII. You shall not steal.

IX. You shall not bear false witness against your neighbor.

X. You shall not covet ...

DAY 22

Leviticus 19:1-8

GOD COMMANDED HOLINESS.

Every good story reaches a point where the main idea becomes clear. Many Bible scholars consider Leviticus 19 the "thematic center" of the book.[1] Others even go as far as to call it the "highest development of ethics in the Old Testament."[2] Today we begin our journey into this important chapter to see what it teaches us about **holiness.**

How would you define holiness? How do you feel about this word?

My prayer is that by the end of today we will all come to appreciate just what "holiness" means. An 18th-century pastor, Jonathan Edwards, once wrote: "Holiness is a most beautiful and lovely thing. We drink in strange notions of holiness from our childhood, as if it were a melancholy, morose, sour, and unpleasant thing; but there is nothing in it but what is sweet and ... lovely."[3]

The original Hebrew word for "holy" means *"set apart."* The *Lexham Cultural Ontology Glossary* defines "holiness" as "moral, social, ritual, and ceremonial purity or innocence."[4] Meaning? Well, moral purity means no sin. Social purity means always loving your neighbor perfectly. Ritual and ceremonial purity have to do with daily living and being set apart, as opposed to being common.

Copy the words from Leviticus 19:2 that the Lord asked Moses to speak to the people of Israel.

Who **is** holy?

Who ***"shall be"*** holy?

We find the same command in 1 Peter 1:15-16. What does it say?

The ancient Israelites found their guidelines for right behavior (and therefore holiness) in the Ten Commandments. Study the chart of the Ten Commandments in your guide. How many of those commandments do we find in our reading for today?

Once again, we find the phrase *"I am the LORD your God"* multiple times in the reading. As a matter of fact, we will see this phrase over 40 times in Leviticus 18-26! Why? Because knowing and believing this truth was essential for the Israelites. It also happens to correspond to which of the Ten Commandments?

Which two commandments do you see mentioned in verse 3?

Which commandment is mentioned in verse 4?

While the Ten Commandments are indispensable, what guidelines did Jesus give for us in Matthew 22:35-40?

Now the text takes a bit of a turn, discussing again the peace offering sacrifice, reminding the people to keep it *"holy to the LORD"* (Leviticus 19:8). This might seem out of place until we stop to think about what holiness really entails. We often think of holiness exclusively as obedience or submission to God's laws and commands. But the truth is, we cannot achieve holiness on our own. We also need communion with God and a reminder of His love and grace. The peace offering was about relationship. It was Israel's reminder that they were once separated from God, but by His mercy, they had peace with Him. The same is true for us today. Holiness involves being in a relationship with God and having a reverence and gratitude for the sacrifice Jesus made to draw us back to Him.

Why do you think a relationship with God is also vital to holiness?

I'm leaving you with a quote that captures the beauty of God and His holiness in a personal way. Bible teacher Jackie Hill Perry says, "If God is holy, then He can't sin. If God can't sin, then He can't sin against me. If He can't sin against me, shouldn't that make Him the most trustworthy being there is?" [5]

Write what you have learned about holiness today.

DAY 23

Leviticus 19:9-18

GOD COMMANDED HOLINESS THROUGH LOVING OUR NEIGHBOR.

Yesterday we talked about holiness. We learned that we, too, are to be holy because God is holy. (Leviticus 19:2) We talked about how God gave ancient Israel "holy guidelines" through the Ten Commandments. Let's start here for today's reading as well.

Which of the Ten Commandments do you see represented in today's verses?

Once again, let's review Jesus' words in Matthew 22:25-30. How did Jesus sum up all of our holiness guidelines?

Yes, holiness is about obeying God's laws and guidelines. But it is more than that. It is also about our relationship with God and how that relationship affects what we do. To be holy is to be set apart for God, and all those who trust in Christ have been made holy by God. Christians are already holy, not because of what we do but because of what Christ has done! God has set us apart as His own. Therefore, living out this reality of being holy means knowing God and therefore imitating Him in all aspects of life.

Reread Leviticus 19:9-18. Remember, the heart behind the law holds so much relevance to us today. God wants us to imitate His heart. As you read, jot down what these laws teach you about God's heart and how it inspires you. (I'll provide you an example to get started: Verses 9-10 show God's love and care for the poor and struggling. He sees them. Therefore, I also want to stop and really SEE those who are struggling around me and provide opportunities for them.)

Let's end today with one simple yet profound thought. **We are most holy when we live loved and live out God's love.**

What does that mean to you?

Take a moment to pray, asking the Holy Spirit to guide you in one area where you can grow in holiness. Record those thoughts here and make a plan on how you can take one step toward that this week.

DAY 24

Leviticus 19:19-37

GOD'S STATUTES GUIDED HIS PEOPLE IN HOLY LIVING.

We have talked a lot about holiness. Today, we'll focus on the remaining verses of Leviticus, where God sets forth statutes (or laws) to guide His people into holy living. As you read through these laws, several might seem strange to us today. Context is vital to understanding the heart behind these laws and therefore what they have to say to us today. I've listed many here, so let's jump right in!

Leviticus 19:19 concerns cross-breeding or cross-pollinating. This was in accordance with ancient Jewish taxonomy. So, for example, they could not breed a sheep with a goat, or cross wheat with barley. Surrounding nations mixed these things together as a magic ritual in hopes that their gods would look favorably upon their crops. Some scholars believe this is why God forbade it for the Israelites. Whatever the reasons are, it is clear that God considered these activities a direct rebellion against the Creator's order. It's also why God required Israel to separate themselves from the surrounding unbelieving, pagan nations.

In what ways might this apply to us today? (See John 17:16-19.)

The next law in verse 19 addressed wearing a garment of mixed materials. According to Exodus 28:5, the priests wore garments of mixed materials (yarn and linen), and according to Numbers 3:10, no outsider from another tribe could attempt to be like a priest. This addresses several issues for us today as well. Just as not everyone was a priest in the Old Testament, not everyone today is a believer or a follower of Christ.

What does 1 Peter 2:9 call us today, as believers in Christ?

Also, just like dressing like a priest wouldn't make someone a priest, acting like a Christian doesn't make one a Christian. God is the one who changes hearts and makes us into a new creation.

Read Isaiah 61:10. According to this verse, who clothes us now? And with garments and robes of what?

Leviticus 19:20-22 caused me some confusion until I uncovered the context behind this law. Let's break it down...

According to Deuteronomy 22:23-24, what happened to a man and woman who had a sexual encounter while she was betrothed to another? (Betrothal in ancient Israel was as good as marriage, even though the couple had not yet consummated their marriage.)

According to Deuteronomy 22:28-29, what was to happen if a man slept with a virgin woman who was not betrothed?

Let's get some context as we study Leviticus 19:20-22. It was common for a "master" to arrange marriages for their female "slaves" ("slaves" is better translated here as "servants"). Fathers arranged almost all marriages, so in this instance, the master acted as father.

The hypothetical situation being described in Leviticus 19:20-22 involved a master who had arranged a marriage for his female servant and sworn an oath to this other man. However, the man had not yet paid the bride price for the betrothal to make it official (which in essence "ransomed" or freed her).

Therefore, when another man slept with the female servant, he wasn't sleeping with a betrothed woman (so no death penalty), but he would have to pay the bride price and marry her. He also heaped on another sin in that he caused the master to break the oath he had sworn to the original suitor. This was the cause for the additional guilt offering.

We might wonder what this has to teach us today. I imagine both the master and the man promised betrothal felt hurt, slighted, embarrassed, etc. Sometimes in our anger, we cry out for maximum punishment on those who hurt us (in this case, death). However, this story reminds us God's judgment is not clouded by emotion like ours.

What does Romans 12:19-21 teach us?

Leviticus 19:23-25 says the Israelites were forbidden to eat from fruit trees in the first three years after planting them. The word for *"forbidden"* (v. 23), *ʿā·rēl,* is actually the Hebrew word for "uncircumcised." This brings to mind the rules for circumcision for a male child, which did not happen until the eighth day after birth. The first three years, the trees were like babies; then they were dedicated to the Lord as first fruits, and then they could be a blessing.

Read 2 Thessalonians 2:13. What does this say about "first fruits"? What is "sanctification"?

Leviticus 19:26-28 deals specifically with pagan practices.

Pagans had rituals involving raw meat. Meat with blood we discussed in Leviticus 17:11, where it said life is in the blood. Jesus' blood (aka life) is the only life we take in. (John 6:54) Predicting the future and contacting dead spirits was another pagan practice, which we see in verse 31. And believe it or not, certain hairstyles or hair cutting were also distinctly pagan. Cutting oneself was another pagan ritual, as was marking oneself, which some English translations have interpreted to the word "tattoos." It is important to point out that these markings were clear pagan symbols on the body.

What was God saying here? And how might that relate to us today?

Another common practice in ancient times was to earn money by "selling" daughters as prostitutes (as daughters seemed to have little value otherwise in ancient cultures). However, the Lord made it very clear by His choice of wording in Leviticus 19:29 that daughters are precious and protected by their heavenly Father!

Leviticus 19:2 says *"Speak to* ***all*** *the congregation of the people of Israel"* and then declares both men and women to be what?

We find one of the few "you shall" statements in this grouping in verse 32. What does it say? And how does it relate to Proverbs 20:29?

Leviticus 19:33-34 addressed strangers and resident aliens. Scholars interpret *"not do him wrong"* (v. 33) to mean "economic exploitation, the deprivation of property, or denial of legal rights." [1] Even more, the law required Israelites to treat others as natives. This chapter also talks about honesty in business. (vv. 35-36) In both cases (the treatment of aliens and fellow Jews alike), God asked His people to remember that they had once been strangers in Egypt, graciously delivered by God.

What similar lesson does 1 John 4:19 teach us today?

Write down one takeaway from today's lesson relevant to your life today.

DAY 25

Leviticus 20:1-9

DISOBEDIENCE HAD SEVERE CONSEQUENCES.

Chapter 20 of Leviticus is going to take a look back at the laws given in Chapters 18-19 and now affix consequences to disobedience.

Within this chapter, God set forth severe consequences to demonstrate the seriousness He attached to His Word. *The New American Commentary* points out that, in ancient Israel, the crimes that received the strongest punishment had to do with crimes of a religious nature or crimes against family life. This was in direct opposition to the other ancient Near Eastern civilizations, where the most severely punished crimes had to do with economic violations (i.e. loss of money, property, etc.). [1]

What might this interesting fact teach us about the heart of God?

Let's dig into Leviticus 20.

The first offense listed is against people who did what? (v. 2)

What was the double punishment? (vv. 2-3)

Molech was an ancient pagan god that some believed could be bought or influenced. They thought the bigger the sacrifice the person made, the more likely Molech would "hear" their request. So, to show the biggest "belief," people would sacrifice and kill their own children. This was a complete abomination to God and should have been for His people as well.

First, what does this teach us about God's heart toward children? (Matthew 19:14) In what ways can you personally act out God's heart toward children in today's world?

Second, before we look down our noses at this ancient society, has there ever been a time when you have tried to treat God as if He were a "Molech" through bribing or "buying" God's ear to hear your request? How does this verse teach us the danger of this?

In Leviticus 20:4, the Scripture also called out all who *"close their eyes"* to such an abominable sin.

Let's just stop here for a moment. Where might there be an injustice or social issue in our world today that is clearly in opposition to the gospel, yet you have been tempted to *"close your eyes"*? Why might that be the case? And what might God be calling you to do on His behalf?

Ancient Jewish society was family driven. Family groups lived close together. It could have been tempting to *"close their eyes"* because they did not want to rat out family. But God is very clear that we cannot choose family over what is right.

What does Matthew 10:37-39 teach?

Leviticus 20:4-5 says that if the people of the land did not deliver the consequences, then God Himself would enact judgment. The same wording is used down below in verse 6 when it references those who attempt to use divination. Often, people would attempt to keep these sins "secret."

Yet what does Numbers 32:23 say?

Therefore, is there such a thing as "secret sin" before God?

Let's look at the final verse in today's reading.

What offense is listed in verse 9?

What was the penalty?

This may appear harsh, but the Hebrew word for *"to curse"* meant to invoke harm. In fact, according to *Faithlife Study Bible*, "Ancient Near Eastern cultures considered curses to be a literal means of inflicting physical harm or death." [2]

But even here, God set a higher standard. While "cursing" (harming) one's parents resulted in death, God's commandment actually stated to do **what** toward parents? (Exodus 20:12) What was the promised result?

Family doesn't come before God, but family is clearly important to God.

Write down one takeaway from today's lesson relevant to your life today.

ESPECIALLY HARD (BUT HOLY) SECTIONS

CAPITAL PUNISHMENT

In Leviticus, God established for the nation of Israel a justice system that invoked specific punishments for sinful behaviors. You may have noticed that the system included death by stoning. To our modern ears, this sounds barbaric. What exactly is going on here, and what can we learn from it?

First, Israel was a theocracy. A theocracy is a government ruled by a divine being. God ruled over Israel as their sole ruler and King. God set in place laws that differed greatly from other nations'. He required high standards of holiness (to reflect a holy God). Because God is holy and perfect, He had every right to save or condemn humanity and do so justifiably.

So does this passage give us a right to capital punishment today? For that, let's look to the New Testament. The New Testament does not explicitly address the issue of capital punishment, but we can glean wisdom from Jesus' interactions. I find Jesus' interaction with the woman caught in adultery relevant to our conversation. The law required stoning for a woman caught in adultery. The religious leaders told Jesus that Moses' law required she be stoned. They then asked Jesus what punishment He would give this woman. Jesus answered, *"Let him who is without sin among you be the first to throw a stone at her"* (John 8:7). And one by one, they all walked away. This leads us to the bigger takeaway from this hard part of Leviticus ...

Passages like this provide a vivid picture for the price of sin. Romans 6:23 says, *"for the wages of sin is death."* And Romans 3:23 makes clear that *"all have sinned."* This means one thing: We all deserve the death penalty. Every one of us. We tend to take sin lightly, but it is serious. Sin, all sin, is an abomination to God. It's an outrage and atrocity to His holiness. So, yes, God is right and just in handing us all the death penalty.

Which is what makes Romans 6:23 so powerful: *"but the free* ***gift*** *of God is eternal life in Christ Jesus our Lord"* (emphasis added). We don't deserve life. But our good God gifts it to anyone who turns and trusts in Jesus. He so graciously made a way. Jesus took our death penalty on Himself. And He gave us His eternal life.

When read in this light, the hard parts of Leviticus become beautiful reminders of what Jesus' sacrifice really means. I deserved death, but He gave me life. How precious is His grace.

Weekend Reflection
WEEK 5

For Week 5, let's take a deeper look into one of the laws we studied in Leviticus 19:9-10. Here, God commanded the Israelites to leave the edges of the harvest in the fields for the poor and the sojourner to reap. Clearly, the Lord had a heart for the poor and the struggling.

But what really fascinates me is the effect this law had not only on a future wealthy bachelor and a poor widow, but on you and me as well. See, there was once a poor, widowed sojourner named Ruth the Moabite. She had traveled with her mother-in-law to a city named Bethlehem, the Scriptures say, *"at the beginning of barley harvest"* (Ruth 1:22b). There lived a man named Boaz who owned fields of grain. Following the law of Leviticus 19:9-10, his reapers left behind some of the grain from the harvest. Ruth went to this field to gather grain. Did this provide physical food for Ruth and her mother-in-law? Absolutely. But there is more to the story ...

Boaz, who simply obeyed God's command not to gather the gleanings after his harvest, and Ruth, one of the people who God intended to protect with the command, eventually married. From this marriage came a baby boy named Obed. Obed was the grandfather of a man named King David. And from the line of King David came our one and only Messiah, Jesus.

Oh, the trickle effect of obedience! Sometimes God's ways feel hard or confusing. Jesus asks us to give until it hurts and lay our future in His hands. Sometimes we might think we look "weird" when we say "no" to the ways of the world. Other times it doesn't feel fair. When we live and love and forgive and give like Jesus, it is not always easy, but friends, it is GOOD. And obedience has a trickle effect. We might not see it this side of heaven, but rest assured, God can take every hard "yes" you give Him and use it to rain down blessings. Obey God, and leave the rest to Him.

WEEK 6

DAY 26

Leviticus 20:10-21

SEXUAL SINS CARRIED ESPECIALLY SEVERE CONSEQUENCES.

In Chapter 18, we studied sexual sin and the guidelines God established. In Chapter 19, we talked about the holiness of God. And today, we examine the consequences of breaking the laws established by a holy God in Leviticus 20.

To begin, read 1 Corinthians 6:18-20 and answer the following questions:

According to this verse, Christians are to flee from what? (v. 18)

Because it is a sin against what? (v. 18)

Our bodies are a what? For whom? (v. 19)

We are NOT what? (v. 19)

Because we were what? (v. 20)

We live in a culture that says, "If it feels good, do it." We are told to follow our hearts and that we can't step in the way of love. And many say that what happens in a person's bedroom is none of our business if no one is getting hurt. However, as Jesus-followers, we live differently. Not in a snooty, look-down-on-others kind of way! But we believe God created us. And as our Creator, He knows what is good for us and has the right to tell us how to live. He is holy (that word again!), and He bought us at a high price: the blood of His one and only Son, Jesus. And because of that, I am His. This body and this heart belong to Him.

Let's keep this in mind as we dive into Leviticus 20:10-21.

To be clear, it appears that the sexual encounter in these verses is consensual, primarily from the fact that both parties receive the punishment. For the offenses listed in verses 10-16, what is the punishment?

Jay Sklar says the severity of the punishment teaches us three things about sin.

1. **SIN IS SERIOUS.** These laws came from the Creator and King and to disobey meant treason.
2. **SIN MUST BE ADDRESSED.** Unaddressed sin is like a disease that grows worse with time.
3. **SIN HAS CONSEQUENCES.** As Galatians 6:7 says, God will not be mocked; we reap what we sow. [1]

How do these three things apply specifically to sexual sin?

According to biblical scholar Warren Wiersbe, 15 offenses warranted capital punishment in ancient Israel.

They were:

STRIKING OR CURSING A PARENT.
(Exodus 21:15; Exodus 21:17)

BREAKING THE SABBATH.
(Exodus 31:14)

BLASPHEMING GOD.
(Leviticus 24:10-16)

ENGAGING IN OCCULT PRACTICES.
(Exodus 22:18)

PROPHESYING FALSELY.
(Deuteronomy 13:1-5)

ADULTERY.
(Leviticus 20:11-12)

RAPE.
(Deuteronomy 22:25)

UNCHASTITY BEFORE MARRIAGE.
(Deuteronomy 22:13-21)

INCEST.
(Leviticus 20:11-12)

HOMOSEXUALITY.
(Leviticus 20:13)

BESTIALITY.
(Leviticus 20:15-16)

KIDNAPPING.
(Exodus 21:16)

IDOLATRY.
(Leviticus 20:1-5)

FALSE WITNESS IN A CASE INVOLVING A CAPITAL CRIME.
(Deuteronomy 19:16-21)

KILLING A HUMAN INTENTIONALLY.
(Exodus 21:12) [2]

As you look over this list, do any of the offenses surprise you? What might this list teach us about what is serious to God?

Leviticus 20:17-21 covers additional sexual sins with a slightly lesser penalty. To be *"cut off"* was to be sent into exile. And to *"die childless"* meant the family name and legacy were to disappear forever. Now that we have studied this section, let's draw a few conclusions.

No one said that being holy was easy. To be like God is hard. It requires a daily "dying" to our flesh and choosing to trust God's way. And we cannot do this on our own. It starts with a relationship with God. It is about admitting that we cannot be holy on our own and accepting Jesus' holiness and sacrifice in our stead. Then our hearts are filled with His love and goodness toward us. And when you know that He chose YOU, He bought you with the blood of His Son and He loves you like crazy, then you can do the hard and holy work of becoming more like Him.

In what ways does holiness feel hard for you? And why might Jesus' love be the key?

Next, it is important we point out that this section of Scripture was written to ancient Israel at the beginning of their covenant relationship with God. He was establishing a people to show the world Himself. Therefore, under this covenant, strict rules were established to teach the truly serious nature of sin. This does not mean that these punishments were meant to be continued today.

Read John 8:1-11. Take a moment to pray and ask for the Holy Spirit's wisdom. Write down what you learn.

DAY 27

Leviticus 20:22-27

HOLINESS REQUIRED SEPARATION.

Today's reading serves as a sort of conclusion to Leviticus 18–20. These three chapters taught us about holiness and what it looks like.

Write down a definition or something new you have learned about holiness so far in this study.

We have talked about the beauty of holiness. It is absolute purity. God is perfectly holy, and we are thankful for it. We have also talked about holiness as a hard thing. God called His people to imitate Him in holiness, and it wasn't possible to do perfectly. Today we return to one of the reasons it was so hard.

Leviticus 20:23 says, *"And you shall not walk in the customs of the nation that I am driving out before you, for they ..."* what?

The Israelites were entering a godless land. A land where no one followed God's ways. They would be completely surrounded by a culture attempting to lure them into unholy ways. Enormous temptations awaited them.

Describe the environment you live in. What specifically about your culture tries to pull you down spiritually?

The Baker Encyclopedia of the Bible says, "... holiness means 'to cut' or 'to separate.' Fundamentally, holiness is a cutting off or separation from what is unclean, and consecration to what is pure." [1] Let's use this definition to illuminate today's reading.

How many times do you see the word "separate[d]" in Leviticus 20:24-26?

God separated Israel from what? (vv. 24, 26)

Similarly, God asked Israel to separate clean animals from what?

Jesus told an interesting parable regarding separation in Matthew 25:31-33. What will Jesus separate here?

However, notice in the definition above that holiness is not just a separation from something but also a consecration to something. Fill in the words from Leviticus 20:26:

"YOU SHALL BE ______________________, FOR I THE LORD AM HOLY AND HAVE SEPARATED YOU FROM THE PEOPLES, THAT YOU SHOULD ________________."

Now let's look at this in terms of the New Testament.

Hebrews 12:14 says without holiness, we cannot what?

That can seem scary because, in and of ourselves, we fail at perfect holiness. However, what does 1 Corinthians 1:30 say? (Read in the NIV also if possible.)

Now read 2 Timothy 1:9.

JESUS' HOLINESS SAVES US AND CALLS US TO LIVE A HOLY LIFE NOT BECAUSE OF ____________ BUT BECAUSE OF ____________ AND ____________ .

Fill in the blank below with something personal:

"IN STRIVING TOWARD HOLINESS, I WILL DO MY BEST TO LIVE A LIFE SEPARATED FROM __________________ AND CONSECRATED TO **JESUS**."

DAY 28

Leviticus 21:1-22:16

PRIESTS WERE CALLED TO A HIGHER STANDARD.

In Leviticus 21-22, we will study the guidelines God established, especially for priests. Priests held positions of leadership. They set the example for holiness in the Israelite community. Therefore, God held them to a higher standard than the rest of the people.

What positions of leadership (both in and outside the Church) do you think are or should be held to a higher standard? Why?

Leviticus 21:1-8 sets forth criteria for priests in both mourning and marriage.

Remember, coming in contact with the dead made a person unclean. What few exceptions did the law allow for a priest regarding coming in contact with the dead?

What did verse 5 forbid? (These are pagan mourning rituals.)

Theologian Warren Wiersbe says, "Even in our grief, we must seek to glorify God." [1] How does 1 Thessalonians 4:13 support this thought?

In regard to marriage, Leviticus 21:7 says a priest could not marry who?

The truth is that our family life affects us. This is especially true for our spiritual life and ministry. What does 2 Corinthians 6:14-16 remind us?

Leviticus 21:9 is a heavy verse, but let's break it down.

A young, unmarried woman caught sleeping around received a severe punishment. What was this punishment, according to Deuteronomy 22:21?

The same would have happened for the daughter of a priest. However, because of her father's high position, the act received a double punishment in that her body was then what (according to Leviticus 21:9)? (By the way, the original Hebrew word *zanah* literally means "to fornicate," and although it is translated by the ESV as "whoring" and translated by the NIV as "becoming a prostitute," the word truly means any sexual relations outside of marriage.)

This was equivalent to being denied a burial or tombstone. This second punishment was directed toward the family of the woman. Why do you think this might have been the case? (A verse like 1 Timothy 3:4-5 may provide some insight.)

Leviticus 21:10-15 addressed the high priest. In mourning, he could not come into contact with a dead body at all. In marriage, he could only marry a virgin from the tribe of Levi. (Remember, his son was to become the next high priest, so lineage was important.) Verse 12 forbids the high priest from leaving *"the sanctuary."* This does not mean that he could never leave the temple but rather that he could not go outside for the purpose of mourning and burying the dead.

Now we reach another especially hard part of our reading. Leviticus 21:16-23 prohibited anyone with a physical disability to offer sacrifices in a priestly manner.

List the disabilities mentioned in this section.

Does this make you uncomfortable? Initially it made me uncomfortable. But the Holy Spirit took me to Jesus and how He constantly loved people with disabilities. And we know today that having a disability in no way disqualifies a person from serving God! When we look at the Apostle Paul, he often mentioned having a *"thorn in [his] flesh"* (2 Corinthains 12:7). Some scholars have speculated this to be some kind of physical ailment, perhaps even an eye condition. And while we do not know for sure his ailment, it is interesting to think that, if it were a physical condition like an eye condition, then according to Leviticus 21:20, even Paul would have been disqualified from priestly service. Yet under the New Testament there is no physical condition that disqualifies us from God's work. So let's talk about what we are seeing here in the Old Testament.

Many scholars agree that the tabernacle (later, the temple) served as a symbol of heaven. God dwelled there in all His perfection. And God wanted the people to see that in His presence was perfection. And this is exactly how it will be, one day, in heaven. There will be no disabilities in heaven. No eyes that can't see, no limbs that can't move, no injuries that won't be healed. I once heard said, "The only scars in heaven will be on Jesus' hands and feet."

Read Revelation 21:2-5. What phrases stand out to you?

It is also important to note that this Leviticus passage in no way suggests that people with physical disabilities be patronized, even in ancient culture. In fact, let's look at verse 22 ...

It says a man from the tribe of Levi with a physical disability could do what? And not just of the holy things, but also of the what? (This was a high honor, like receiving a seat at the king's table and sharing in his food.)

Leviticus 22:1-16 instructed priests in how to treat and guard the holy things.

As we've seen, priests held an important role that carried with it many rules and much responsibility. They were in charge of *"holy things"* and had to maintain a seriousness and respect for such things. How might this be similar to the words in James 3:1?

Leviticus 22:10-16 assigned the priests the task of guarding the holy things from lay people. To offer holy, set-apart things to a person for whom they were not intended was to bring sin upon that person. The priest's job was to help with atonement for sin, not add to sin. How is this similar to the words given to leaders in Acts 20:28?

Finally, take a moment today to pray for spiritual leaders you know. Pray for strength, courage and character. Pray for their families as well.

DAY 29

Leviticus 22:17-33

THE QUALITY OF THE OFFERING MATTERED.

When it came to sacrifices, quality mattered. Let's jump right in.

Leviticus 22:20 forbade the people from offering what?

Read Malachi 1:8 and verses 13-14. What do you learn about the people's attitude in bringing blemished animals? Why was this not acceptable?

What particular aspect of being holy (like Jesus) are you tempted to find wearisome? What would Galatians 6:9 remind us today?

It would have been tempting to cut corners, maybe try to sneak in a slight blemish. Maybe God knew that some people would try to push the boundaries, wanting to see exactly how much they could get away with. Isn't that human nature? And yet these laws weren't written to be a list to follow. The intent was to check the condition of their hearts.

Read a short moment about King David in 2 Samuel 24:24. What heart-revealing question did he ask?

How might this apply today?

We find great emphasis on a perfect, unblemished sacrifice in today's reading. This is so important. Why? Because that perfect sacrifice pointed to another perfect, unblemished sacrifice ...

What words of 1 Peter 1:19 describe the precious blood of Jesus?

If you have a big heart for animals, the Old Testament sacrificial system might be difficult to appreciate. From the moment sin entered the world, all of creation has suffered the consequences. This includes the first recorded animal sacrifice, when God sacrificed an animal to clothe the Adam and Eve to cover their shame. (Genesis 3:21)

Even though it may seem God didn't value animals, I'd like to close this lesson by showing God does value and have a heart for animals.

Let's start with today's reading. Leviticus 22:27-28 gave what two specific rules regarding animals? Scholars cite this as an act of compassion. It also helped teach His people to respect life.

In Genesis 9:8-10, notice that God established a covenant with Noah but also with what?

The last verse of the book of Jonah is super interesting. Jonah 4:11 says God took pity on the city of Nineveh because of the 120,000 people and also because of what?

What interesting law does God give in Deuteronomy 22:6-7?

What does God say in Psalm 50:10-11?

Jesus talks about God's care for people by using the illustration of God's care for which animal in Matthew 6:26?

Finally, Isaiah 11:6-9 gives us a tiny glimpse into heaven. What animals do you see listed?

How can you help love and care for God's creation today?

ESPECIALLY HARD (BUT HOLY) SECTIONS

PEOPLE WITH DISABILITIES

When you are, or someone you love is, a person with disabilities, Leviticus 21:16–23 can feel confusing and even painful. Taken out of context, this section can perpetuate an atmosphere of looking down on or feeling pity toward people with disabilities. However, like all parts of the Bible, we must study this text in its larger context of the Bible as a whole.

The very best place to begin is Psalm 139:13–16, which says:

"For you formed my inward parts; you knitted me together in my mother's womb. I praise you, for I am fearfully and wonderfully made. Wonderful are your works; my soul knows it very well. My frame was not hidden from you, when I was being made in secret, intricately woven in the depths of the earth. Your eyes saw my unformed substance; in your book were written, every one of them, the days that were formed for me, when as yet there was none of them."

Every single person has been crafted and formed by God, and every one of them is "wonderful." Disabilities do not define a person. Each person has been specifically and beautifully formed. When studying Leviticus 21, it's easy to focus on what the priests with disabilities could not do instead of focusing on what they could. God still valued them and assigned them priestly duties. He also allotted them food from the offering (something that the majority of people could not receive). Scholars have set forth different theories as to why God established this rule; none feel particularly comforting. Perhaps the most convincing theory is that priests who had disabilities could not perform the same sacred duties as other priests to show us that there will be no disabilities in heaven. In God's Kingdom, all will be healed, and the tabernacle and the priestly system are meant to be a picture of that reality. We gain valuable insight when we examine the larger place that disabilities hold in the Bible.

It is substantially clear that having a disability does not in any way disqualify a person from God's greater mission. Job developed a disabling condition that led his friends to tell him he had sinned or that he should curse God. But he never wavered in his faith, even with his questions. (Job 12:3-4; Job 12:13) There are some Torah scholars who suggest that Isaac had developmental delays. [1] We know he was blind toward the end of his life. (Genesis 27:1) God gave Jacob a *"limp"* (Genesis 32:31). Leah's *"eyes were weak"* (Genesis 29:17). Moses possibly had a speech impediment. (Genesis 4:10) Some scholars suggest King Saul suffered from bipolar disorder. [2] We know Mephibosheth, a contemporary of King David, had a mobility disability. (2 Samuel 4:4) In the New Testament, God blinded the Apostle Paul for a time. (Acts 9:9) Even after regaining his sight, Scripture tells us he suffered with something he called *"a thorn"* in his side (Galatians 6:11; 2 Corinthians 12:8-9). Some believe it was an eye condition. And yet God allowed all these people to share an important part in God's story. Each one made significant and valuable contributions. In some cases, God reversed the disability, but certainly not always. In fact, you could argue that Paul never saw more clearly than when he was rendered unable to physically see.

By looking at the complete narrative of the Bible, we learn disabilities in no way discredit a person from being a valuable, needed part of God's mission. God has given every single one of us a unique assignment to further the beautiful, colorful, diverse Kingdom of Christ.

DAY 30

Leviticus 23:1-8

GOD ESTABLISHED HOLY DAYS.

I have a giant whiteboard calendar that hangs next to our back door. Every month, I fill it up with the many activities, practices, meetings, social gatherings, holidays, birthdays — on and on the list goes. Calendars and clocks keep our lives moving and provide rhythms. Some days are filled with work, and some days are marked for rest. There are days set aside to remind us to love, to honor our veterans and even to care for the earth. Such rhythms and moments are vital to being human, and it was God Himself who established the idea from the beginning of creation. Today we'll study two of the holy days that God established for ancient Israel.

Leviticus 23:2 discusses the appointed feast days for Israel — days God asked Moses to declare *"holy convocations."* We have defined this word *"holy"* a lot throughout this study. What do you think Moses' declaration said to the Israelites about these established days?

Let's look at the first holy day established ...

Leviticus 23:3 allowed the Israelites to work for six days, but what must they do on the seventh? This was called what?

Read Genesis 2:1-3. What do we learn here?

Many benefits flowed from this set-aside day. First, it served as a constant reminder of the creation story. Why might it be a blessing to have a weekly reminder that God created everything we see?

The Sabbath also helped protect the land and kept the people from exploiting it, as we will later see in Chapter 25. We can also see in today's society that businesses and industries are often tempted to get ahead by exploiting either their resources or their employees. Why is this not OK with God?

The Sabbath was also God's gift and blessing to mankind. This would have been especially true for this group of ancient Israelites who had just left a life of slavery in Egypt, where they received no rest. What does Jesus say about the Sabbath in Mark 2:27?

An interesting fact: In 1929, the Soviet Union attempted to put an end to the weekend. They called it *nepreryvka*, or "continuous working week." In an effort to maximize workforce efficiency and productivity, the Soviet Union established a calendar that grouped everyone by occupation. A person was required to follow the calendar, working five days in a row, followed by a day off. The next day, that person started his or her five-day work cycle again. The government also staggered all the occupations to ensure that industry never fully stopped. But this made it so that families and friends didn't have the same off days. They couldn't spend time together. It also (intentionally) made it difficult for people to attend religious services, as no one could attend the same days. After 11 years, this system proved to be an utter failure. [1]

Why do you think *nepreryvka* failed? What are we reminded of today about God's ways?

Under the New Testament, we no longer observe the strict Sabbath of the Old Testament.

What does Colossians 2:16-17 say? And what does Mark 2:28 say about Jesus?

While we no longer observe a technical Sabbath, what might we learn from this Sabbath idea, both about God and about ourselves?

Let's move to the second holy day in today's reading.

In Leviticus 23:5, what holy day is established? And what immediately followed it in verse 6?

Let's read about the very first Passover in Exodus 12:16-27 and make a few observations ...

According to Exodus 12:17 and 12:27, the feasts were meant to remind the Israelites of what event?

I love the line in Exodus 12:26. What question do the children ask?

What was done with the Passover lamb? (vv. 21-23)

Let's use these observations from Exodus to make a few conclusions today.

In Leviticus 23:5, it says this took place in which month of their year? How do you start your year?

What holidays, rituals or traditions does your family practice throughout the year that have a particular meaning for you?

We are going to look into this in much more detail in our Weekend Reflection, but it is vital to point out the importance of Passover to Christianity. Passover foreshadowed (pointed forward to) the Passover Lamb. What does 1 Corinthians 5:7 say about the Passover Lamb?

Weekend Reflection

WEEK 6

For Week 6, let's take a deeper look into Passover. Passover will come to hold a special place in the hearts of Christ-followers if we take in the wonder and beauty of how it points to Christ.

Interestingly, the end of Jesus' life happened near the time of Passover and the Feast of Unleavened Bread. (Matthew 26:17) In fact, the last meal Jesus shared with His disciples was the Passover meal.

In the first Passover, recorded in Exodus 12, God required the sacrifice of an unblemished lamb to serve as a sign to protect His people from the angel of death that would "pass over" their homes. God wanted His people to remember this monumental event of salvation, so He established a feast called the Feast of Unleavened Bread. It required the Israelites to remove all leaven from their homes for seven days. In 1 Corinthians 5:7, it says, *"Cleanse out the old leaven that you may be a new lump, as you really are unleavened. For Christ, our Passover lamb, has been sacrificed."* It later describes our *"unleavened bread"* as *"sincerity and truth"* (1 Corinthians 5:8).

At the first Passover, God commanded the people to apply the blood of the lamb to the doorposts of their houses with hyssop. In his crucifixion account, Jesus' disciple John remembered a fascinating detail. When Jesus hung on the cross, the soldiers offered Him sour wine. How did they lift it to Him? On a hyssop branch. (John 19:29) However, Jesus refused. He was making a new way.

In Exodus 12:23, we learn that the blood of the Passover lamb smeared on their doors saved the Israelites from death. The Lord's judgment was about to strike the Egyptians, but the lamb's blood prevented *"the destroyer"* from entering the Israelites' homes.. The blood of Jesus does the same for us. First Thessalonians 1:10 says Jesus saves us from *"the wrath to come."* We do not have to fear death because Jesus Himself said, *"I give them eternal life, and they will never perish, and no one will snatch them out of my hand"* (John 10:28).

How amazing to see that, almost 1,500 years before Christ came, God symbolically presented His plan to the world. And here we are now, over 2,000 years later, living in humble gratitude for God's plan in action: Jesus Christ, the Lamb that was slain to save His people forever.

WEEK 7

DAY 31

Leviticus 23:9-25

GOD ORDAINED THE FEASTS OF THE FIRSTFRUITS, WEEKS AND TRUMPETS.

Oh, friends, I am excited for today's reading, which is rich in symbolism and meaning. These three feasts were meaningful for ancient Israel, but just wait until you see what they mean for us today!

THE FEAST OF THE FIRSTFRUITS

Leviticus 23:10 commands the people to bring a sheaf of the what of their harvest?

According to verse 14, God forbid them to do what until they made this offering?

According to verse 11, when was this to take place? (If Sabbath was on what we consider to be Saturday, what day of the week was this?)

For ancient Israel, this was a dedication of their harvest. The very first part of the harvest was given to God before they could have a taste of it.

What does Proverbs 3:9 say?

Now what does this mean for Christians today?

According to 1 Corinthians 15:20, Paul refers to Jesus as the *"firstfruits"* of what? And it is because He did what?

When did this happen, according to Matthew 28:1-6? (What day of the week?)

Jesus is the firstfruit so that we might also have what? (See also 1 Thessalonians 4:14.)

THE FEAST OF WEEKS

Before we go into this next feast, I want to take a moment to study the use of the number seven. God often gives numbers in the Bible symbolic significance. The number seven is one of those numbers. The Hebrew word for seven (*sheba*) represents completeness and perfection. God completely and perfectly created the world in seven days. The all-important Sabbath fell on the seventh day. In addition to "completeness," the Hebrew word *sheba* is closely related to another Hebrew word, *shaba*, which means to swear an oath.[1] As Bible scholar Warren Wiersbe puts it, "Whenever the Lord 'sevens' something, He's reminding His people that what He says and does is complete and dependable."[2]

With this in mind, let's discover when the Feast of Weeks took place. According to Leviticus 23:15, the Feast of Weeks took place how many weeks after the Feast of the Firstfruits? (The reason verse 16 says *"fifty days"* is if the person was counting from the Sabbath before the Feast of the Firstfruits.)

In the years following the Jewish post-exile period, and as the Greek language became more prevalent, this feast underwent a name change. Its new name came from the Greek word *pentēkostē*, which literally means "fiftieth day." In English, we call this Pentecost.

What holy day took place in Acts 2:1?

Now read Acts 2:2-4. Describe what happened. Who came to believers?

Imagine for a moment what this means. Seven weeks after Jesus was resurrected (or seven sevens ... "completely complete"), came the birth of the Church and the ushering in of the Holy Spirit.

What sticks out to you about this symbolism? What might it teach us about God?

THE FEAST OF TRUMPETS

The author of Leviticus explained these feasts in chronological order as they would have happened through the year. Let's review. Jesus' resurrection fulfilled the Feast of Firstfruits. The Feast of Weeks pointed to the birth of the Church. Interestingly there is a four-month gap between the Feast of Weeks and this next feast, the Feast of Trumpets. Wiersbe suggests that this gap could represent the age we are in now, the "age of the church," where we eagerly await the "sound of the trumpet." [3]

What might Matthew 9:36-38 have to say about what our role should be in this age?

Not much is written in Leviticus 23 about the Feast of Trumpets, but let's take a look.

According to Leviticus 23:24, in what month did this take place? (Just in case you are curious, this falls on our calendar somewhere around September or October.)

And how did they proclaim this day?

Jews still celebrate this particular holy day today. It is known as "Rosh Hashanah" and viewed as a "new year" day on their calendar. Jews regard this as one of the two "High Holy Days." (We will look at the second tomorrow). The Jews blow a ram's horn (or *shofar*) on this day. The "trumpet" blast is interesting. Numbers 10:1-10 explains the three reasons for blowing the trumpet ...

What was the first reason for the trumpet sound? (Numbers 10:2)

What was the second? (Numbers 10:9)

What was the third? (Numbers 10:10)

Let's see what this means today ...

According to 1 Corinthians 15:52, what will the last trumpet sound mean?

How about in Revelation 11:15-18?

How does this final trumpet sound achieve all three purposes for a trumpet, as found in Numbers 10?

DAY 32

Leviticus 23:26-32

THE DAY OF ATONEMENT WAS TO BE TREATED SERIOUSLY.

Yesterday we learned that modern-day Jews have two "High Holy Days." One is Rosh Hashanah, which is equivalent to the Feast of Trumpets. The second is called Yom Kippur, and it is a nod to the Old Testament Day of Atonement. Let's review what we have already learned about the Day of Atonement.

Read Leviticus 23:26-32. When did this holy day take place?

According to verses 27, 29 and 32, what did the Lord require of His people? Note: The word "afflict" did not mean God was commanding the people to injure themselves in any way, but rather it was a call to absolute fasting and confession.

We studied the Day of Atonement in detail in Leviticus 16. Let's go back for a quick review. (You can find your notes on Day 18 of this study guide.)

The Day of Atonement was the one day a year that the high priest could go where? (Leviticus 16:2-3)

According to Leviticus 16:30, what was the purpose of this day?

Hebrews 9 teaches us that Jesus is our "Day of Atonement." He is the better High Priest, and He entered the better "Holy Place," namely, the **heavenly** throne room of God Himself! His sacrifice covered, once and for all, our sin and shame. In Him, we stand clean.

Knowing this, what word comes to mind as you reflect on Jesus' finished work on the cross? Why that word?

Jews today celebrate Yom Kippur differently than in ancient days. They no longer offer animal sacrifices with blood sprinkled on altars. More recent Jewish tradition states that, during the 10 days between Rosh Hashanah and Yom Kippur, God will decide the fate of each individual and whether they are written in the "book of life." According to History.com, "As a result, observant Jews consider Yom Kippur and the days leading up to it a time for prayer, good deeds, reflecting on past mistakes and making amends with others." [1]

While these are noble pursuits, how does Christianity differ, according to Titus 3:5-7?

Going back to our text in Leviticus, let's end on one final thought.

What was the punishment for not fasting or for doing any work on the Day of Atonement? (Leviticus 23:29-30)

God intended the punishment as a reminder of the holiness of God and of this set-apart day. Today, how might you set aside a moment of holy respect for the sacrifice your Savior, Jesus, made for you?

DAY 33

Leviticus 23:33-44

THE FEAST OF BOOTHS WAS ABOUT REJOICING BEFORE THE LORD.

When I was little, my favorite thing ever was to go camping in the mountains. I packed my Cabbage Patch sleeping bag, a warm jacket and marshmallows for hot chocolate. What more could a little kid want? Now that I'm older, I have a slightly different view of camping, especially when it comes to sleeping outdoors on the ground for fun. Ha!

How do you feel about camping? What might be the best, and worst, parts?

Today we study the final feast of Leviticus 23, the Feast of Booths. A little like a camping trip, this feast moved the people out of their homes and their comfort zones to help them regain perspective.

First, in what month of the year did this feast take place? And how many days did it last? (Leviticus 23:34) As we learned a couple of days ago, what does this number symbolize?

According to verse 40, what did God ask the people to cut down?

According to verse 42, what did God ask them to build?

Fill in the blanks with Leviticus 23:40-41a:

"... AND YOU SHALL ________________ BEFORE THE LORD YOUR GOD SEVEN DAYS. YOU SHALL ________________ IT AS A FEAST TO THE LORD FOR SEVEN DAYS IN THE YEAR."

Palm branches played a big part in the Feast of Booths. Let's travel to the New Testament to see where else we find palm branches.

What is taking place in John 12:12-13?

How about Revelation 7:9?

John 1:14 tells us Jesus *"became flesh and dwelt among us."* The Greek word for "dwelt," *skēnoō*, literally means "to pitch a tent."

How is Jesus' coming to earth similar to "pitching a tent"?

Zechariah 14:16 gives us a look into worship of God after Jesus' life, death and resurrection.

According to this verse, people of surrounding nations will gather together to worship the King and Lord of hosts. This verse also likens that worship of God to what?

I imagine seven days sleeping in a booth would make you grateful for your bed and the roof over your head. This festive time was filled with family and rejoicing and food and sacrifices. I have heard it said (and it has become a motto my family now lives by) that sometimes we need a change of pace and a change of place to gain a change of perspective.

In what ways might you or your family benefit from a change of pace or place? In what ways do you need a change of perspective regarding life and God? And what step can you take today to make that happen?

FEASTS OF LEVITICUS

Spring Holidays

- **PASSOVER** — JESUS' DEATH
- **UNLEAVENED BREAD**
- **FIRST FRUITS** — RESURRECTION
- 50 DAYS
- **WEEKS (PENTECOST)** — HOLY SPIRIT

Fall Holidays

- **TRUMPETS**
- **DAY OF ATONEMENT**
- **BOOTHS**

DAY 34

Leviticus 24:1-9

THE LIGHT AND THE LOAVES REPRESENTED GOD'S CONTINUAL PRESENCE.

Yesterday we finished our look into the feasts and holy days established by God to continually remind the people to turn to God. Today we'll learn how the tabernacle's lamp and bread served as daily reminders of God's presence in their lives.

Find the illustration of the tabernacle layout in your study guide. Find the lampstand and the table for the bread.

Which room in the tabernacle contained these items?

Let's examine each one separately.

LIGHT

Leviticus 24:1-4 gave the instructions regarding the lamps in the tabernacle.

Read Exodus 25:31-33. Describe the lampstand. (Today this lampstand style is called a *menorah*, a common symbol in Judaism. Can you sketch out a basic shape?)

Back to Leviticus 24:1-4: How many times do you see the word "*regularly*"? (In the NIV, the word used is "*continually*.")

You might remember an old motel commercial with the slogan "We'll leave the light on for you." When the lights are on, someone is home, awake. The continual light in the sanctuary reminded the people that God was always "home." His presence was always with them. The regular care to tend the light also reminded them that they should continually love and serve the Lord.

What does it mean to you that God "leaves His light on" for you? He is always home, always present, always awake.

What does Jesus say about Himself in John 8:12?

Revelation 1:12-16 gives us a glorious picture of Jesus. What images of light do you see?

LOAVES

Leviticus 24:5-9 gave the details regarding the bread for the tabernacle.

Read Exodus 25:23-29. Describe the table used for the bread.

What is the bread placed on the table called in Exodus 25:30?

Back to Leviticus 24:5-6: How many loaves were to be made? How much flour was in each loaf? And how were they arranged on the table?

(This fact astounded me: The bread would have been baked in flat, unleavened loaves. Since they were flat, they could be stacked, which was essential because the table was small and these loaves were large, weighing at least 5.6 pounds [or 2.6 kilograms] **each**.[1])

The 12 loaves represented the 12 tribes of Israel. The bread was constantly before the presence of the Lord. Each Sabbath, the Lord required Aaron to set out fresh bread. Eating a meal (breaking bread) together signified the sealing of a covenant between people in ancient culture. The priests eating the bread signified sealing the covenant between God and His people.

Because of Jesus, we, too, have the ability and privilege of continually coming before God. According to Hebrews 7:25, how do we draw near to God?

What does Jesus say about Himself in John 6:35?

In Matthew 26:26, Jesus used bread as a symbol to remind us of what?

DAY 35

Leviticus 24:10-23

THE LAW ESTABLISHED THAT PUNISHMENTS SHOULD FIT THE CRIME.

Today, our reading takes an interesting turn. Suddenly, we find ourselves in the middle of a narrative regarding a situation that arose while the law was being established. This situation led to an important legal principle that we are going to dig into as well. Let's start with the story.

What was the heritage of the guilty man in Leviticus 24:10-11? And what crime did he commit? (The capital "N" on "Name" let's us know this means God's Name.)

Which of the Ten Commandments did this violate? (Exodus 20:7)

When violated, the Ten Commandments carried with them extreme punishments. List the punishments for worshipping false gods. (Leviticus 20:2) Adultery? (Leviticus 20:10) How about cursing your father or mother? (Leviticus 20:9)

Initially, what did the people of Israel do to this particular offender? (Leviticus 24:12)

This is important. God was establishing a nation as well as both a legal and justice system. And just like today, the people were not sure how to apply the law in unique situations. Because the man in question wasn't entirely Jewish, they had to determine whether Israel's laws applied to him. Placing him in custody was the right thing. Instead of making any assumptions about what God would want, they stopped. They sought the Lord. And they waited for His answer.

While we are no longer under the ancient Israelite legal system (and aren't you glad?!), what lesson might we learn from their response?

I found it interesting that part of the punishment required the people who heard the blasphemy to go and lay their hands on his head. (Leviticus 24:14)

Where have we seen this image before? (See Leviticus 4:29 as an example.)

The New American Commentary states that "The hearing of a blasphemous statement rendered one culpable." [1] This means they also bore condemnation or blame. Could it be that blasphemy, a total and utter disrespect for the Lord, is so dangerous that it can affect the hearts and minds of anyone who even hears it? If so, what might this have to teach us?

This incident in Leviticus 24 led to the establishment of a very important legal principle. In Latin, it is called *"lex talionis"* or "law of retaliation." In plain English, it means the punishment must fit the crime.

Read Leviticus 24:17-22 to gain a clear understanding of this law. Chances are, you have heard this referred to at some time. Was it used in love? Or anger?

Indeed, many have misunderstood and abused these verses through the years. However, it is important that we note two things:

First, this illustration demonstrated an important legal principle for the nation. Even in our world today, this legal principle remains. Why might *lex talionis* be vital for legal systems?

The first hopefully leads us to the second important note, and that is that this legal principle, while sounding harsh to our modern ears, was intended to ensure justice and compassion in determining punishments. It kept people from abusing power or crushing the weak for the smallest offense. In other words, small crimes could ONLY receive small punishments. It served to keep the peoples' thirst for greater revenge in check.

Try rereading Leviticus 24:17-22 with a compassionate, legal perspective. Does it seem different? Why or why not?

We know today that we are not under ancient Israelite law. We are, however, under the laws of our own respective nations. And hopefully these laws are just and fair. However, as Christians, we submit to an even higher law. As citizens of heaven, we follow our King, Jesus. What did Jesus have to say about this law in Matthew 5:38-42? What does this mean to you?

Weekend Reflection

WEEK 7

For Week 7, let's take a deeper look into the punishment for blasphemy. Leviticus 24 told us the story of a man found guilty of blaspheming God's name. (v. 11) The punishment for his crime, and therefore anyone who followed in his footsteps, was to *"surely be put to death"* (v. 16a). Why? Because it was a serious infraction that held an equally serious consequence.

When Jesus began His ministry, many didn't love and welcome Jesus. Most especially the religious leaders. They refused to accept what He said. It infuriated them that crowds of people followed Him. Jesus threatened their power and control. They wanted Him dead. And do you know how they did it? They used the law and punishment for blasphemy. At Jesus' trial, Matthew recorded the following account:

"Then the high priest tore his clothes and said, 'He has spoken blasphemy! Why do we need any more witnesses? Look, now you have heard the blasphemy. What do you think?' 'He is worthy of death,' they answered" (Matthew 26:65-66, NIV).

Surely this moment played through God's mind centuries before when He established the law against blasphemy in Leviticus. He knew people would use this law against His own Son, yet He still set it in place. Why? Maybe because it is true. And God can speak nothing but truth. Blasphemy is a terrible sin in a long list of terrible sins all deserving of death. Sin deserves death. Which means we deserve death. But it is also why Jesus came to *"set [us] free ... from the law of sin and death"* (Romans 8:2). Oh, praise Him for that!

I find it telling that, even though God knew His Word would be used against His own Son, He still gave us the Truth. For ages, people have weaponized Scripture for their own personal agendas. They hold tight the passages they want, and disregard others. They see only what they choose, and thereby form God into their own image. But wrongful interpretation and application by man does not make God wrong! And any time man twists the good word of God to hurt or belittle the people God loves, God is not honored or pleased. This is why a correct and careful approach to studying God's Word is so important. Lord, help us not to misinterpret Your Word and Your heart!

WEEK 8

DAY 36

Leviticus 25:1-22

THE SABBATH AND JUBILEE YEARS ESTABLISHED SOCIAL, ECONOMIC AND THEOLOGICAL PRINCIPLES.

In Leviticus 24, we studied various legal principles God established for His nation. Today, we will learn about other societal principles that were to be at the heart of the nation of Israel. These principles stand out when we examine God's commands on Sabbath and Jubilee years. Even though we do not follow these principles today, we can still glean wisdom from them and what they teach us about our good and holy God.

SABBATH YEAR

In Leviticus 25, God established a Sabbath year. What year was this supposed to take place? (v. 4)

What jobs specifically could not be done this year? (vv. 4-5)

Did you notice these were agricultural jobs? Therefore, other types of work could be done during this time. But the agricultural rest is an interesting concept.

Ancient farming practices were particularly backbreaking jobs that required many hands. Who in particular might this Sabbath have benefited?

Tilling, harvesting and carrying food to markets would have also required animal labor. What else benefited from this Sabbath?

And according to Leviticus 25:5, this Sabbath year was particularly a solemn rest for what?

As both a farmer's daughter and a farmer's wife, I have learned a few things about agriculture. And a good farmer will tell you that one of their main jobs is to take care of the land, which allows the crops to grow. Farmers have long seen the benefits of crop rotation, so as not to wear out the land or rob it of its important nutrients. But of course, God knew this from the very beginning. I love seeing how much God cares for all of His creation, from people and animals and plants to even the dirt on the ground.

What part of creation has God given you a heart toward? How might you join Him in caring for it today?

JUBILEE YEAR

In Leviticus 25:8-9, God established a year of Jubilee. This took place every how many years? ("*Seven weeks of years*" in verse 8 means seven times seven.) And it happened in what month of that year? (v. 9)

The word "jubilee" in Hebrew is *yôbēl*, which refers to a ram's horn that could be used for a trumpet.[1] It is possible it got this name because what was supposed to happen on the day the Jubilee year started? (v. 9)

Verse 10 says in this year the people were to proclaim what?

"Liberty" means "freedom" or "release." This was a release from debt or indentured servanthood.

According to verse 10, people were then free to return to what two things?

There are so many interesting factors that took place with this year of Jubilee. Freeing people and releasing debts, allowing people to return back to their families and their family land, truly provided a fresh start once every generation. From a social standpoint, it established the importance of family. Family units were literally put back together every 49 years. From an economic standpoint, it prevented a feudal system from taking place. A feudal system was where there were many poor serfs who were serving a small number of extremely rich landowners. From a theological standpoint, these years of Sabbath rest, especially the Jubilee year, required such a step of faith! As with Sabbath years, (v. 5) Jubilee year meant no crop could be planted or harvested. (v. 11) Can you imagine giving away a year's salary every seven years? And as if that was not difficult enough, once in your lifetime you would need to give away your salary two years in a row (Sabbath and Jubilee year were back to back)! To follow and obey God's command in this was the ultimate sign of covenant loyalty and trust.

What principles can we apply today when we look at the year of Jubilee from a societal standpoint? How about from an economic standpoint? Theological?

Does God want to be involved only in the religious parts of your life? (Hint: The answer is no!) Why not?

Let's look at one final aspect of these rest years. I love this quote from Jay Sklar. He says, "The picture that emerges takes us back to Eden: people living securely in God's garden, having all their needs met, and walking in obedient fellowship with the Lord. This has always been the Lord's intent for humanity." [2]

And the best part is that someday it will be like this again! (Hebrews 4:4-11)

What excites you about the rest that awaits us in heaven?

DAY 37

Leviticus 25:23-34

GOD PROVIDED A WAY FOR THOSE WHO FELL ON HARD TIMES.

Yesterday we looked at the Jubilee year. This law ensured debts were erased and people returned back to their families and land. However, what happened if a person fell on hard times in between those years? God anticipated that as well.

Let's start with a subtle line in today's reading that has huge implications. In Leviticus 25:23, God says, *"The land shall not be sold in perpetuity, for..."* what?

Think of everything that "belongs" to you. Do you have land? A house? A car? What about a degree? Or a job? A boss, an assistant or even employees? Do you have a pet? Children? A spouse? Friends? Neighbors? ALL of these things actually belong to whom?

Yet in verse 24, God did allow His people to have ownership of His possession. It was theirs to care for, love, nurture and develop for Him. How well do you steward what the Lord has given you? Does this reminder that all we have belongs to God change your mindset or care? Why or why not?

Sometimes "life happens," and we lose the thing we have been entrusted with.

Leviticus 25:25 addresses what happens if someone becomes what? And, therefore, they had to do what to their part of their property?

Why might a person fall into hard times?

Hard times sometimes result from our own choices, from the choices of others or just plain bad circumstances. (This is a fallen world.) Yet no matter the cause, God made a path for that person to help them climb out.

The first way was to have a what? (Leviticus 25:25)

The word "redeemer" is the Hebrew word *g*^{e}*’û·lîm*. The writer of Isaiah uses a similar word to describe God in Isaiah 63:16. Write down the last line of this verse as your own declaration to God.

The second way out of hard times was to what? (Leviticus 25:26)

The third way was to wait until what? (Leviticus 25:28)

In verses 29-31, different rules applied depending upon where a person lived — out in the country or within a walled city. A house in the country was tied to the land and therefore the family. Homes in town were not. The rules were also different for Levites. God gave the priests 48 cities in the promised land where they could live. Why did God make this special exception? Because Scripture tells us the Lord was their *"portion"* and *"inheritance"* (Numbers 18:20).

Let's draw a few conclusions. If you were an ancient Israelite who fell on hard times, a redeeming kinsman could help you out, you could work your way out or you could wait for the Lord's Jubilee year.

Are we, as Christians today, promised a pass from hard times? (See John 16:33.)

What might the heart of this Leviticus passage teach us today regarding hard times?

DAY 38

Leviticus 25:35-55

ISRAELITES WERE ONLY TO BE SERVANTS OF GOD.

Throughout the book of Leviticus, we have seen how God set His holy standard. And parts of that have been hard. It's why we've worked hard to put the laws into historical context. But it's also necessary to fit them into the context of the Bible as a whole. This is particularly vital for our reading today, which addresses the subject of slavery. First, we will examine the text. Second, we will give our text historical context. Finally, we will look at how this topic fits in the Bible.

The first part of Leviticus 25:35 addressed Israelites' indebtedness to other Israelites.

According to verse 36, they were to try and help each other out without taking what?

If, for some reason, it was the only option that remained (in other words, the only thing of value they owned was themselves), the individual could *"sell himself"* to cover the debt. How was the "buyer" to treat that person? (v. 40)

All of this between Israelites was because of one very important fact, found at the end of the section. According to verse 55, Israelites were *only* supposed to be servants (which is the same Hebrew word used for "slaves") to whom?

However, this standard for indebtedness did not apply to non-Israelites.

According to verse 44, God allowed the Israelites to buy who from the nations around them?

Verse 45 says "*... and they may be your ...*" what? What thoughts go through your mind when reading this?

Are you wrestling with this text? If so, this is good! It is so very sad that some in history have used this text to justify slavery in the eyes of God. And here is where the correct study of Scripture is so important.

First, let's look at historical context, beginning with a language lesson. You may wonder why we so often go back to the original language. But contemporary language is a funny thing, always shifting and moving. Translations give us the essence of the original language, but at times, because it is a translation of the original language, we can be left missing some of the nuances of the original words. This sometimes leaves us with a flat image instead of something three-dimensional. So it is with the Hebrew word *ebed*. The word *ebed* could mean "servant," "indentured servant," "permanent servant" or, yes, "slave." It could also mean an ugly form of slavery, like what the Israelites experienced in Egypt. But *ebed* did not necessarily mean brutal slavery. When we use the term "slave" today, we picture the horrible slavery of the Greco-Roman empire and, in more recent times, that of the United States of America. Our definition of "slave" is someone who is kidnapped or born into captivity, forced against their will to work for no wages or compensation, who is seen and/or treated as less than human and therefore given no rights. This slavery is wrong! And it is not the *ebed* that Leviticus mentions.

According to Exodus 21:26-27, what would happen if an *ebed* was abused?

According to Exodus 20:10, an *ebed* also had the right to what?

Another difficult concept here is when we read *"slaves"* were called the *"property"* of another person (Leviticus 25:45). That term is dehumanizing in today's context. However, as Jay Sklar points out, we actually often use commercial language to refer to people. Sports teams "trade" players like stockbrokers trade stocks. Companies "transfer" employees like they transfer money. [1] So while the term "property" today triggers many emotions and feelings (and rightly so because of the harsh and cruel treatment enslaved people in the United States and elsewhere experienced under such terms), the intent of this ancient biblical term was different. *In the context of their world,* it reminded the Israelites that these people (still human beings made in the image of God) were now their responsibility to care for. In a sense, the word changed the nature of the relationship and required the Israelites to reflect to others the care and kindness that they experienced from God.

In what ways do we care for the people under us like we care for the things in our possession? (Obviously, there are also many ways that our care for people should also be different from our care for possessions. Name a couple of these as well.)

I want us to be clear. We do not want to glaze over the hard parts. It is true that the Bible does not come right out and condemn slavery. But let's travel to the New Testament to see what it has to say.

What does Peter express in Acts 10:34-35?

What does Galatians 3:28 say?

Read 1 Timothy 1:9-10. Who (related to today's topic) is listed among those especially evil sinners? Who are specifically addressed in Colossians 3:22-24 (and thereby seen as important people to God)?

What interesting words do you find in 1 Corinthians 7:21-24?

In Philemon verses 16-17, Paul tells Philemon to welcome back his former slave, Onesimus, not just as a slave but as a what?

Read Ephesians 6:5-9. Commands are given to both slave and master. According to the last sentence of verse 9, which one is more important to God?

Today's study has certainly been both holy and hard. Take a minute to sit with the Lord today. Bring Him your questions and ask Him to reveal to you His heart and love for all people.

ESPECIALLY HARD (BUT HOLY) SECTIONS

SLAVERY

On Day 38, we talked about the Hebrew word *ebed*. An *ebed* was a servant, or, as is commonly translated, a "slave." The historical and biblical context shows that this was not the kind of slavery that we necessarily think about when we hear that word today. For us, slavery brings to mind the horrible practice of forcing people of color to work without pay and treating them as less-than, resulting in the abuse and exploitation of image bearers of God. Leviticus opened our eyes to the hard and holy parts of the law. Today, we will examine some hard and not-so-holy parts of Church history to remind ourselves once again how important it is to correctly study and apply Scripture.

The Atlantic slave trade began in the 1440s. Mariners from Portugal sailed to Africa, kidnapped human beings, and forced them to Europe for personal gain and profit. As this brutal industry increased, Pope Nicolas V decided to make an official Church stance. He condoned slavery if the slave owners "converted" their slaves to Christianity. He granted permission for Europeans to, in his exact words, "invade, search out, capture, vanquish, and subdue all Saracens and pagans whatsoever ...[and] to reduce their persons to perpetual slavery ... and to convert them to his and their use and profit ..." [1] And so began the lie that God justified slavery because it converted souls to Christ. Never will God justify sin. Kidnapping, physically and verbally abusing, and oppressing people made in the image of God is sin. And while God can certainly bring good, such as salvation in Jesus, out of an evil situation, a holy and just God never applauds the means of sin to reach this end.

When settlers brought enslaved Africans to the U.S., many American Christians, following the example of the Europeans, justified slavery using the Bible. They used passages like the ones found in Leviticus to validate slave owning, arguing because Israel had "slaves," slavery must be acceptable. They also cited the passages from the New Testament telling slaves to obey their masters as further "proof." While few slave owners cared about the spiritual well-being of enslaved people, there were a few who allowed slaves to attend church (segregated from white "masters"). These slavery proponents also often intentionally left out certain biblical texts, especially the book of Exodus, where God's people marched out of slavery. How dangerous it can be to pick and choose scriptures we like and agree with, and disregard those we do not!

We do find light in this time of darkness for people of color. As some enslaved people experienced God's Word, it came alive in their hearts. The pages of Scripture being used to oppress them actually introduced them to a God of love, freedom and equality. What a reminder that, no matter who tries to weaponize God's Word for their own benefit or agenda, the true message of God's Word will always be there, waiting for those who truly seek Him.

Today, as a Church, we can take a moment to see the very imperfect past. We can own up to the mistakes and resolve to never use the Bible as a way to justify our means to an end. We can take steps forward to right the wrongs and seek reconciliation. We can focus on simply being more like Jesus.

IF YOU'D LIKE TO READ MORE ABOUT THIS TOPIC, SEE OUR ENDNOTES SECTION ON PAGE 208 FOR A LIST OF RECOMMENDED RESOURCES.

DAY 39

Leviticus 26:1-46

GOD SET CONDITIONS FOR HIS BLESSINGS AND PUNISHMENT.

Within Leviticus 26, we find quite a few "if, then" statements. We call these "conditional statements." **If** certain conditions are met, **then** the result will be XYZ. It was actually very common in the ancient Near East to close treaties with conditional statements of blessings (if the conditions were kept) and curses (if the conditions were violated). [1] Therefore, this chapter is like a formal closing of the covenant God established between Himself and Israel. It is so important as we begin that we point out this was a covenant between God and Israel. These promises applied to this particular nation as a whole and were not directed toward individual people.

IF OBEDIENCE, THEN BLESSING

The first conditional statement we see is **IF** Israel did what ... ? (Leviticus 26:3)

... **THEN** what would happen? Name just a few outcomes. (vv. 4-13)

These blessings look a lot like "wealth, health and success." Some people want to use this section to say God will provide such things if you have enough faith and follow Him. However, let's put it into context. Historically, this covenant was between God and Israel alone. This was also a means of officially ending a contract. Let's examine this covenant in its biblical context ...

The Bible does not always promise physical blessings for obedience. In fact, what did Jesus say in John 16:33? The first "blessing" promised in Leviticus 26 is rain. (v. 4) Yet what does Jesus say about God in Matthew 5:45?

That is not to say this passage is completely irrelevant today. We find biblical principles in the New Testament that teach us that making good, godly and wise choices leads to a better life. (Galatians 6:7b-8) But moreover, Leviticus 26 actually builds toward a special blessing in verses 11 and 12.

What is the blessing?

Friends, John 1:14 tells us that blessing has arrived! Who is that blessing?

How is this the best and only promise we need?

IF DISOBEDIENCE, THEN PUNISHMENT

Leviticus 26 moves on to say that **IF** Israel did what ... ? (vv. 14-15)

... **THEN** what would happen? Just broadly name a few outcomes ... (vv. 16-39)

Again, not every calamity in life is punishment from God. We live in a fallen world where famine, war and disease are part of sin's curse. But in the course of His covenant with Israel, God did often employ extreme measures to keep His nation on mission. The mission was too important for them to fail! Let's study the five stages of punishment and warning here ...

The First Stage (vv. 16-17)

What were some of the consequences?

The Second Stage (vv. 18-20)

If they didn't respond and obey, then what would happen?

The Third Stage (vv. 21-22)

What crazy thing came here?

The Fourth Stage (vv. 23-26)

If the people still rebelled, what then?

The Fifth Stage (vv. 27-39)

What was the final punishment?

Friends, I know this can be really hard to take in. So much anger and wrath. I don't know about you, but I don't always enjoy studying this side of God. It can feel scary. It can also be easy for us to get caught up in the severity of the punishments here and forget to focus on the bigger picture.

When you were a kid, how many warnings did you get from your parents or guardians before you were disciplined for doing something wrong? How many warnings do you think we should give criminals? Yet look again at this list. How many times did God attempt to get the nation's attention and set them on the right path?

It is at times like these when I also need to be reminded of the words in Psalm 103:8 and 2 Peter 3:9. What do these verses say?

But I also don't want us to get too cozy with this section of Scripture. As we have seen, holy is both good and hard! And the truth is that God DOES get angry. Sin is not OK with Him. Honestly, it is not OK with us either. It is good that God hates sin. And God's mission was too important to let Israel self-destruct in sin. That is why these consequences came about. Israel (which eventually split into Israel and Judah) was eventually captured by foreign enemies and scattered among the nations. God was true to His word, which means Jesus wasn't messing around when He spoke these strong words in Matthew 13:41-42.

What does Jesus say and what does it mean to you?

But the text doesn't stop here, friends. We find one more major conditional statement in Leviticus 26 that we should note.

Verse 40 says, *"But **if** they ..."* what?

Verse 42 says, ***"then** I will* ______________________ *..."*. The same is true for us today. What does 1 John 1:9 say?

ESPECIALLY HARD (BUT HOLY) SECTIONS

PROSPERITY GOSPEL

It might be tempting to look at Leviticus 26 as a form of prosperity gospel. Prosperity gospel is a perversion of the gospel that suggests the full realm of physical, earthly blessings (namely wealth, health and power) is available to those who come to God and either act in obedience, demonstrate enough faith or give a sizable enough monetary contribution. At first glance, the text in Leviticus 26 might seem to imply that following God indeed leads to "health and wealth." It might also seem to promote that disobeying God leads to curses or bad things happening to you. This then leads to thinking that *Perhaps if I don't do bad things, then bad things won't happen to me* (which is simply the flip side of the same prosperity gospel coin). Let's examine the text, as well as what the Bible as a whole has to say about the theology of prosperity.

We learned that ancient Near East covenants often ended with blessings and curses. (It was also especially common to end documents during this time with far more curses than blessings.) These were considered "conditions" of the agreement. In a similar way, Leviticus 26 reveals God's intentions for His people. His heart's desire for us is peace, safety, abundance and ultimately fellowship with Him. At the same time, a life apart from God will look dark and scary, indeed.

The difference between us and ancient Israel is that **Israel was a momentary picture of eternal things.** The ultimate goal of life is not (and truly never was) meant to be wealth and health. In fact, Paul calls this life we live now a *"light momentary affliction"* (2 Corinthians 4:17). Christ Himself says in this life we *"will have tribulation"* (John 16:33). We find no promise of wealth and health in this life. But there is the promise of Christ. And in the hard times, the suffering of this life, we discover Christ is enough. In truth, we have something better than ancient Israel ever had, even when the nation was at its height of wealth! His name is Jesus. The Israelites were looking forward to their Messiah, but we get to look back to Him. We also have the hope, the promise, that someday this life will be over, and the next life will graciously provide us with everything we could ever want or imagine. All of God's good desires for us will come true in heaven. We will not use and abuse them for selfish pleasure or gain (think about that for a moment!), but instead we will give them back to the One who gave them. We will place them at the feet of our very good Savior.

Leviticus 26 is not meant as a goal to lust after in this life but a picture of what God intends for the life to come.

DAY 40

Leviticus 27:1-34

GOD KEPT HIS WORD AND HE EXPECTED HIS PEOPLE TO DO THE SAME.

Friends, we have reached our last day together in the study of Leviticus! Studying this book has truly been hard and holy work. And from our time together, we have learned how the laws and rituals of Leviticus have given us a glorious glimpse into God's heart. His unchanging, intentional, patient, loving, grace-filled heart. Leviticus ends with God wanting His people to know that He keeps His word, and He expected them to do the same. Let's take a look.

Leviticus 27:2 says,

"IF ANYONE MAKES A ____________ ____________ TO

THE ____________ ..."

Vows were a means of voluntarily dedicating something to God that was above and beyond the normal sacrifice requirements. In fact, what does Deuteronomy 23:22 say about vows?

But if they did make a vow, they should do so how? (Deuteronomy 23:23)

And why was this the case? (Deuteronomy 23:21)

Have you ever made a rash promise that you later regretted, not just with God but with another person? Why might we be tempted to make a promise in the moment? Why might it be difficult to keep later on?

Vows to God did not have to be made, but if they were made they certainly had to be kept! Not to do so was a sin. But we all sometimes promise things and then circumstances change. God understood this, so even though He gave no leniency regarding keeping a vow, He did allow for substitutions (namely, money).

Here are some commonly made vows:

PEOPLE

It was not uncommon for an Israelite to dedicate himself or a family member to the Lord. (See this week's Weekend Reflection!) Once dedicated, the person then served in the tabernacle alongside the priests. Temple work encompassed many kinds of tasks, including heavy manual labor (think of the animals, wood for fires, etc.!). So when we read about the "price" assigned to a dedicated person, this price does not reflect that person's value as a human being but rather reflects the work and wages they would have provided. Also, this was no small vow. Based on the calculations in this passage, the cost of a male between ages 20-60 would have been four years' income! [1] These were certainly not vows to be made rashly.

Read Jesus' words in Luke 14:28-33. What does Jesus say about counting the cost to follow Him?

ANIMALS

A few interesting points on dedicated animals. If someone dedicated a clean animal to the Lord and then decided to dedicate a different animal instead (probably one of lesser value), then the priest would keep both. God is not to be mocked. An unclean animal could be given to the priests (and while the unclean animal couldn't be eaten, it could be used for transportation or sold by the priest). Unclean animals could be redeemed (for money) if necessary.

What might it suggest about human nature that we always, throughout history, tend toward manipulating or cheating the system?

INANIMATE OBJECTS

A person could also dedicate (or vow) his house or land. The priest set a value for the house or land. Actually, the land belonged to the Lord, so the priest valued only the crops. Again, rash vows carried consequences. If a person vowed land they could not financially redeem by the Jubilee year, it would become a permanent part of the priesthood and would be lost to the former landowner and their family forever.

How serious was God about keeping vows? Do you feel you have the same regard for keeping your word? Why or why not?

A FRIENDLY REMINDER

What if one day your boss took a cut of your paycheck, wrapped it up in a nice box and bow, and handed it to you, calling it a "special raise"? Would you feel honored? Of course not! She gave you what was already yours! God applied this same principle at the end of Leviticus 27. God forbade vows for firstborn animals, the tithe or "devoted" things. This would also be referenced later in Israel's history when God commanded them to "devote" their enemies and the spoils of war to Him by completely destroying them. These items/people could not be dedicated to the tabernacle. These items already belonged to God in the first place.

What does 2 Corinthians 9:6-8 remind us about the heart of giving?

As you think back over the last eight weeks, all 27 chapters of Leviticus, think about one new concept, principle or truth that you've learned about God. In what ways have you grown closer to Him?

Were you surprised by how much the book of Leviticus applies to your life today? Why or why not?

Weekend Reflection
WEEK 8

For Week 8, let's take a deeper look into the vows people made to God. In Leviticus 27, we learned that God always keeps His word, and He expected His people to do the same. It might seem odd for someone to vow another person to the Lord, but we find an example of this in 1 Samuel 1.

In 1 Samuel, we meet a woman named Hannah. Hannah was barren and was abused by another woman for it. Her overwhelming sadness brought her to the steps of the temple, where the scriptures say she *"vowed a vow"* (v. 11) to dedicate her first son, if it was God's will to give her such, to the Lord's work. Indeed, a short time later, Hannah gave birth to a bouncing baby boy named Samuel. And verse 24 says that while *"the child was young,"* Hannah brought him to the temple, to a priest named Eli. And then she did what I can only imagine made her heart ache: She left him there. She kept her vow, and she walked away. I wonder if Samuel called out to her as she turned the corner, wondering where his mother was going. What a difficult vow for Hannah to keep!

And yet ... our God also made a vow. He made a vow that He would bless all the families of the earth. (Genesis 12:3) And God kept that vow. He gave **His** own Son. He put Jesus on a cross and then walked away. He heard His Son cry out from that cross, *"My God, my God, why have you forsaken me?"* (Matthew 27:46). Can you imagine that moment?! But God kept His Word. And so Jesus became the sacrifice, the last sacrifice, that every Levitical sacrifice foreshadowed. He covered our sin. And then defeated it forever when He rose from the dead and ascended into heaven. Indeed, friends, the whole earth has been blessed. Every single one of us has the opportunity to call Jesus our Savior and our friend.

So, a vow. Not something to be taken lightly. You had to count the cost. You had to know what you were getting into and be ready to follow through. And that's exactly what God did. Jesus Christ is living proof that God always keeps His Word — yesterday, today and forevermore.

NOTES

10 VERSES

IN CASE YOU WERE WONDERING

Sometimes there is more to understanding Scripture than originally meets the eye. That's why our team wanted to provide you with additional information on some of the most popular verses from Leviticus.

"BUT IF HE CANNOT AFFORD A LAMB, THEN HE SHALL BRING TO THE LORD AS HIS COMPENSATION FOR THE SIN THAT HE HAS COMMITTED TWO TURTLEDOVES OR TWO PIGEONS, ONE FOR A SIN OFFERING AND THE OTHER FOR A BURNT OFFERING." (LEVITICUS 5:7)

This verse is included among a list of sins and offerings in Leviticus 5. However, when compensation for sin was due, it was not based on the sinner's preferred option. It was based on God's requirement.

And yet verse 7 introduces a compassionate provision for those who were poor: *"But if he cannot afford a lamb,"* two turtledoves or pigeons could be brought to the priest to make atonement for the person's sin. When we realize our guilt and seek His forgiveness with a true heart, God gives us grace — regardless of our status in society or the depth of our sin.

In the Old Testament, after the sin offering was made, the burnt offering followed. It expressed thanks and praise to God. But it also foreshadowed the praise we can offer Him since Christ, our Great High Priest, became the sin offering for us once and for all. (Hebrews 7:22-27) He is the sinless Lamb of God, who takes away the sins of the world. (1 John 1:29)

JOY WILLIAMS

"AND FIRE CAME OUT FROM BEFORE THE LORD AND CONSUMED THE BURNT OFFERING AND THE PIECES OF FAT ON THE ALTAR, AND WHEN ALL THE PEOPLE SAW IT, THEY SHOUTED AND FELL ON THEIR FACES." (LEVITICUS 9:24)

The priesthoods of the Sumerian, Mesopotamian and surrounding cultures in the ancient Near East developed out of a desire to satisfy their respective deities in works-based religions. The priests offered sacrifices to appease their gods in what was an impersonal relationship. They had no real way of knowing whether or not their sacrifices pleased their gods.

But the priests of Israel acted as intermediaries for the people of God. Sacrifices were made to cover sin so God's people could draw near to God in a personal relationship. As Aaron sacrificed the sin and burnt offerings on behalf of the people, God demonstrated His presence and acceptance in a powerful way. The One True God consumed Aaron's sacrifice.

Today Jesus Christ is our priest and intermediary between us and God. The sacrifices God requires are no longer slain animals but sacrifices of praise from a surrendered heart.
The Bible says that now we, too, are a royal priesthood chosen by God to declare the praises of Him who called us out of darkness into marvelous light. (1 Peter 2:9)

DENISE PASS

"AND AARON SHALL LAY BOTH HIS HANDS ON THE HEAD OF THE LIVE GOAT, AND CONFESS OVER IT ALL THE INIQUITIES OF THE PEOPLE OF ISRAEL, AND ALL THEIR TRANSGRESSIONS, ALL THEIR SINS. AND HE SHALL PUT THEM ON THE HEAD OF THE GOAT AND SEND IT AWAY INTO THE WILDERNESS BY THE HAND OF A MAN WHO IS IN READINESS. THE GOAT SHALL BEAR ALL THEIR INIQUITIES ON ITSELF TO A REMOTE AREA, AND HE SHALL LET THE GOAT GO FREE IN THE WILDERNESS." (LEVITICUS 16:21-22)

When God gave the Israelites this statute for the Day of Atonement, He gave them a visual reminder each year of a live goat bearing their sins and being cast out into the wilderness. This is where we get our English word "scapegoat" — someone who takes the blame for the mistakes of others. God was introducing the people to the idea of a substitute who would bear the sins of another.

The prophet Isaiah later foretold that the Messiah would fulfill this role when He bore the sins of the people: *"All we like sheep have gone astray; we have turned—every one—to his own way; and the LORD has laid on him the iniquity of us all"* (Isaiah 53:6). Even though Jesus was guiltless, sinless and blameless, He bore our sins on the cross and took the punishment our guilt deserved. As 1 Peter 2:24 says, *"He himself bore our sins in his body on the tree, that we might die to sin and live to righteousness. By his wounds you have been healed."*

MARISSA HENLEY

"YOU SHALL NOT TAKE VENGEANCE OR BEAR A GRUDGE AGAINST THE SONS OF YOUR OWN PEOPLE, BUT YOU SHALL LOVE YOUR NEIGHBOR AS YOURSELF: I AM THE LORD." (LEVITICUS 19:18)

The list of rules given to Israel was intended to show them how to live in community with each other. The Lord called them to holiness because He is holy, and He wanted them to be set apart. How could they distinguish themselves and their God among the pagan nations if they exhibited the same violence, idolatry and division? The command to *"love your neighbor as yourself"* summed up many of the Lord's instructions and was a foundational principle for Israel. (Leviticus 19:18; Romans 13:9) James referred to it as *"the royal law"* (James 2:8). And Jesus reinforced this teaching in Matthew 22:37-39 as part of the greatest commandment. When we serve our friends and neighbors and seek the welfare of our community, it fosters peace, trust and unity. Everyone benefits when we treat one another with love and respect.

KELLEY BROWN

"FOR THE LIFE OF THE FLESH IS IN THE BLOOD, AND I HAVE GIVEN IT FOR YOU ON THE ALTAR TO MAKE ATONEMENT FOR YOUR SOULS, FOR IT IS THE BLOOD THAT MAKES ATONEMENT BY THE LIFE." (LEVITICUS 17:11)

Ancient cultures knew that if an animal lost all its blood, it died. They therefore saw blood as its life force. We sing about Jesus' blood in our worship songs, but if we are honest, we don't really like the thought of blood. It reminds us that our flesh is not eternal. Death looms large in the reality that we are temporary. But our eternal God made a way for us to live forever.

The cost of sin is death. (Romans 6:23) There is no way around it. Blood is the only thing that can atone for (cover) our sins. In a system of sacrifices that God set up for man's sins to be covered, God's people brought animals to be slain to make atonement for their sins. The life of one (animal) was given for another (human). Blood rituals were also performed by other neighboring people groups at the same time, but they were offered in ignorance to false gods. God's offering system brought life and forgiveness — temporarily. These sacrifices led to God's ultimate offering of His own Son. Jesus gave His own perfect life and blood in exchange for ours. One sacrifice for all. Through His death we now live forever.

DENISE PASS

"YOU SHALL NOT MAKE ANY CUTS ON YOUR BODY FOR THE DEAD OR TATTOO YOURSELVES: I AM THE LORD." (LEVITICUS 19:28)

At first, this seems like an odd command. Why would the Lord include tattoos and body harming in a lengthy list of do's and don'ts for the Israelites as they came into the promised land? There's a good reason. These, along with sex rituals, were unholy practices of the Canaanites who worshiped a sun and moon god and goddess. It was God's desire for His people to be set apart from all other people groups so they would remain faithful. They were to give themselves fully to the Lord, to follow Him and worship Him only. Choosing to conform to neighboring cultures' traditions and practices was a step in disobedience toward idol worship.

In essence, their actions revealed if the Israelites followed the One True God or the gods of the surrounding cultures. Perhaps that's why, after giving commands such as the one above, God reminded His people, *"I am the LORD"* (Leviticus 19:28). Our Father wants our whole devotion today, too. Although we experience abundant grace as we continually navigate cultural idols, God's Word is clear: He is the only one to follow.

ANDREA CHATELAIN

"AND YOU SHALL NOT WALK IN THE CUSTOMS OF THE NATION THAT I AM DRIVING OUT BEFORE YOU, FOR THEY DID ALL THESE THINGS, AND THEREFORE I DETESTED THEM." (LEVITICUS 20:23)

God gave specific instructions to His people to prepare them for their entry into the promised land. The Lord chose Israel as His own, setting them apart from all other nations. He had given them His laws in order that they might *"dwell in the land securely"* (Leviticus 25:18). Following God's laws always leads to blessing. God's people were not to live like the current inhabitants of Canaan. The Canaanites were sexually immoral idol-worshipers who sacrificed their children to their inanimate god, and YAHWEH *"detested"* these people (a word that means to be grieved, to feel a loathing or abhorrence or sickening dread). YAHWEH's people were to be holy in their beliefs and their behavior, worshiping only Him and abstaining from any kind of sexual impurity. The laws God gave His people at Mount Sinai were not suggestions; they were written in stone — unchanging and unbending. But even in this stern warning, we see God's steadfast love for Israel, despite their own sinfulness, as He reaffirmed His commitment to bring His people into His land.

MARISSA HENLEY

"FRACTURE FOR FRACTURE, EYE FOR EYE, TOOTH FOR TOOTH; WHATEVER INJURY HE HAS GIVEN A PERSON SHALL BE GIVEN TO HIM." (LEVITICUS 24:20)

Leviticus 24:20 may read as a bit brutal, but if we dig into the true meaning behind this passage, we discover it's actually meant to be quite merciful. An eye for an eye, and a tooth for a tooth, isn't a guideline for exacting personal vengeance; it's a legal concept called *lex talionis* designed to be carried out by a fair judicial system. The Latin term *lex talionis* means "law of retribution," and it was set in place to ensure that punishment could not exceed the crime.

While this would sometimes be carried out literally in the Old Testament — such was the case when a murderer then had to lose their own life (Numbers 35:31) — many scholars believe it mostly functioned as more of a generalization for fair compensation. (Exodus 21:18-19; Exodus 21:26)

Ultimately, these words that feel extreme were meant to end vigilante extremes while simultaneously bringing about justice.

KIMBERLY HENDERSON

"AND I WILL WALK AMONG YOU AND WILL BE YOUR GOD, AND YOU SHALL BE MY PEOPLE." (LEVITICUS 26:12)

The concept of belonging suggests that who we are is connected to whose we are. In this verse, God clarifies that we belong to Him and He belongs to us. That belonging expands into togetherness as He says He will walk among us. The same word used for "walk" in Leviticus 26:12 is used to describe how He walked with Adam and Eve in the garden. (Genesis 3:8) We know that God once again walked the earth with us in Christ (John 1:14) and He intends to dwell together with us forever in heaven. What a joy to know that God wants to be with us and that He has chosen us. He promised covenant connection and relationship with us because of His great love for us. May we continue to walk with Him all the days of our lives.

QUANTRILLA ARD

"EVERY TITHE OF THE LAND, WHETHER OF THE SEED OF THE LAND OR OF THE FRUIT OF THE TREES, IS THE LORD'S; IT IS HOLY TO THE LORD." (LEVITICUS 27:30)

When God brought the Israelites into the promised land, He didn't give an inheritance of land to all 12 tribes. God told the priestly tribe of Levi that He Himself was to be their portion and their inheritance. (Numbers 18:20) But with no land of their own, how would the Levites grow food to feed their families?

The Lord provided for the Levites' physical needs by directing the other 11 tribes to give a tenth of everything gained from their lands. (Numbers 18:21; Numbers 18:24) As the Levites received this offering, they themselves also gave a tenth in worship back to God. (Numbers 18:26)

Jesus reminds us of the importance of giving back to God. (Matthew 25:35-40; Luke 6:38; Acts 20:35) As we receive, let us seek God for a willing heart of worship that readily offers our resources so that we may participate in God's purposes in this world.

BETHANY RUTH

END NOTES

As with all sources cited in our publications, Proverbs 31 Ministries does not necessarily adhere to all views by the authors listed in this guide. We have simply found some of their content helpful and encourage our readers to read them critically as you would other sources.

LEVITICUS IN CONTEXT

[1] "Context." *Cambridge English Dictionary*, Cambridge University Press, 2021, https://dictionary.cambridge.org/us/dictionary/english/context. Accessed May 2021.

THE THREE USES OF THE LAW

[1] Robinson, Jeff. "Of What Use is the Law? Three Purposes." *Founders Ministries*. https://founders.org/2014/11/24/of-what-use-is-the-law-three-purposes/. Accessed May 2021.

WHAT YOU MIGHT DISCOVER FROM STUDYING LEVITICUS

[1] Sklar, Jay. "4 Things That Happen When You Study Leviticus More Than 10 Years" *The Gospel Coalition*. https://www.thegospelcoalition.org/article/four-things-happen-when-study-leviticus-ten-years/. Accessed May 2021.

[2] @timkellernyc (Timothy Keller). "If your god never disagrees with you, you might just be worshiping an idealized version of yourself." *Twitter*. 12 September 2014, 12:00pm. https://twitter.com/timkellernyc/status/510458013606739968.

MENSTRUATION

[1] Jones, Rachel. *A Brief Theology of Periods (Yes, Really)*. United Kingdom: The Good Book Company, 2021. pp. 76.

HOMOSEXUALITY

[1] Allberry, Sam. *Is God anti-gay?* India: The Good Book Company, 2020. pp. 80-81.

DISABILITIES

[1] "Famous Figures from History and Today With Disabilities." *The Board of Rabbis of Southern California*. https://www.boardofrabbis.org/files/Heroes_with_Disabilities.pdf. Accessed May 2021.

[2] Stein, George. "The case of King Saul: did he have recurrent unipolar depression or bipolar affective disorder?" *The British Journal of Psychiatry*, Volume 198, Issue 3. March 2011. pp. 212. As seen at Cambridge University Press Online. https://www.cambridge.org/core/journals/the-british-journal-of-psychiatry/article/case-of-king-saul-did-he-have-recurrent-unipolar-depression-or-bipolar-affective-disorder/CE7DBD20965E98FC29A2445C0E620DAD. Accessed May 2021.

SLAVERY

[1] "Pope Nicolas V and the Portuguese Slave Trade." *Lowcountry Digital History Initiative*. https://ldhi.library.cofc.edu/exhibits/show/african_laborers_for_a_new_emp/pope_nicolas_v_and_the_portugu. Accessed May 2021.

INTERESTING LEVITICUS FACTS: ĂZĀʾZĒL

[1] Rooker, Mark F. *Leviticus* (Vol. 3A). Nashville, TN: B&H Publishers, 2000. pp. 216-217.

DAY 1

[1] Moseley, Allan. *Exalting Jesus in Leviticus*. Christ-Centered Exposition, edited by David Platt, Daniel L. Akin, and Tony Merida. Nashville, TN: B&H Publishing Group, 2015. pp. 12.

[2] Swanson, J. *Dictionary of Biblical Languages with Semantic Domains : Hebrew (Old Testament)* (electronic ed.). Oak Harbor: Logos Research Systems, Inc., 1997.

[3] Moseley, Allan. *Exalting Jesus in Leviticus.* Christ-Centered Exposition, edited by David Platt, Daniel L. Akin, and Tony Merida. Nashville, TN: B&H Publishing Group, 2015. pp. 11.

DAY 3

[1] Rooker, Mark F. *Leviticus* (Vol. 3A). Nashville, TN: B&H Publishers, 2000. pp. 102.

DAY 5

[1] Brockway, D. *Atonement.* In J. D. Barry, D. Bomar, D. R. Brown, R. Klippenstein, D. Mangum, C. Sinclair Wolcott, ... W. Widder (Eds.), The Lexham Bible Dictionary. Bellingham, WA: Lexham Press, 2016.

[2] ibid.

WEEKEND - WEEK 1

[1] Moseley, Allan. *Exalting Jesus in Leviticus.* Christ-Centered Exposition, edited by David Platt, Daniel L. Akin, and Tony Merida. Nashville, TN: B&H Publishing Group, 2015. pp. 23.

DAY 7

[1] Sklar, Jay. *Leviticus: An Introduction and Commentary.* (D. G. Firth, Ed.) (Vol. 3). Nottingham, England: Inter-Varsity Press, 2013. pp. 122.

DAY 10

[1] Wiersbe, Warren W. *Be Holy: Becoming "Set Apart" For God.* OT Commentary: Leviticus. Colorado Springs, Co: David C Cook, 1994. pp. 44-45.

DAY 11

[1] Moseley, Allan. *Exalting Jesus in Leviticus.* Christ-Centered Exposition, edited by David Platt, Daniel L. Akin, and Tony Merida. Nashville, TN: B&H Publishing Group, 2015. pp. 95.

[2] Hartley, John E., *Leviticus.* WBC. Dallas: Word, 1992. pp. 126

DAY 12

[1] Sklar, Jay. *Leviticus: An Introduction and Commentary.* (D. G. Firth, Ed.) (Vol. 3). Nottingham, England: Inter-Varsity Press, 2013. pp. 159.

DAY 13

[1] Sklar, Jay. *Leviticus: An Introduction and Commentary.* (D. G. Firth, Ed.) (Vol. 3). Nottingham, England: Inter-Varsity Press, 2013. pp. 172.

DAY 14

[1] Keil, C. F. and F. Delitzsch, *Joshua, Judges, Ruth.* Grand Rapids: Eerdmans, 1970. The Pentateuch, Biblical Commentary on the Old Testament 1–3. Grand Rapids: Eerdmans, 1988. pp. 376.

[2] Moseley, Allan. *Exalting Jesus in Leviticus.* Christ-Centered Exposition, edited by David Platt, Daniel L. Akin, and Tony Merida. Nashville, TN: B&H Publishing Group, 2015. pp. 131.

[3] ibid.

DAY 15

[1] Sklar, Jay. *Leviticus: An Introduction and Commentary.* (D. G. Firth, Ed.) (Vol. 3). Nottingham, England: Inter-Varsity Press, 2013. pp. 183.

DAY 17

[1] Rooker, Mark F. *Leviticus* (Vol. 3A). Nashville, TN: B&H Publishers, 2000. pp. 203.

[2] Rooker, Mark F. *Leviticus* (Vol. 3A). Nashville, TN: B&H Publishers, 2000. pp. 204.

DAY 19

[1] Sklar, Jay. *Leviticus: An Introduction and Commentary.* (D. G. Firth, Ed.) (Vol. 3). Nottingham, England: Inter-Varsity Press, 2013. pp. 218.

[2] Wiersbe, Warren W. *Be Holy: Becoming "Set Apart"* For God. OT Commentary: Leviticus. Colorado Springs, Co: David C Cook, 1994. pp. 95.

DAY 21

[1] Sklar, Jay. *Leviticus: An Introduction and Commentary.* (D. G. Firth, Ed.) (Vol. 3). Nottingham, England: Inter-Varsity Press, 2013. pp. 240.

DAY 22

[1] Moseley, Allan. *Exalting Jesus in Leviticus.* Christ-Centered Exposition, edited by David Platt, Daniel L. Akin, and Tony Merida. Nashville, TN: B&H Publishing Group, 2015. pp. 180.

[2] West, J. *Introduction to the Old Testament.* New York, NY: Macmillan, 1971. pp. 156.

[3] Edwards, Jonathan. *The Works of Jonathan Edwards.* Volume 13. New Haven: Yale University Press, 1994. pp. 163.

[4] Witthoff, D. (Ed.). *The Lexham Cultural Ontology Glossary.* Bellingham, WA: Lexham Press, 2014.

[5] Allen, Jennie, host. Perry, Jackie Hill, guest. *"A Deep Talk about Holiness."* Made for This Podcast. Podcasts app, season 7, episode 22. April 15, 2021.

DAY 24

[1] Sklar, Jay. *Leviticus: An Introduction and Commentary.* (D. G. Firth, Ed.) (Vol. 3). Nottingham, England: Inter-Varsity Press, 2013. pp. 252.

DAY 25

[1] Rooker, Mark F. *Leviticus* (Vol. 3A). Nashville, TN: B&H Publishers, 2000. pp. 265.

[2] Barry, J. D., Mangum, D., Brown, D. R., Heiser, M. S., Custis, M., Ritzema, E., ... Bomar, D. *Faithlife Study Bible* (Exodus 21:17). Bellingham, WA: Lexham Press, 2012, 2016.

DAY 26

[1] Sklar, Jay. *Leviticus: An Introduction and Commentary.* (D. G. Firth, Ed.) (Vol. 3). Nottingham, England: Inter-Varsity Press, 2013. pp. 261.

[2] Wiersbe, Warren W. *Be Holy: Becoming "Set Apart"* For God. OT Commentary: Leviticus. Colorado Springs, Co: David C Cook, 1994. pp. 104.

DAY 27

[1] Elwell, W. A., & Beitzel, B. J. "Holiness" In *Baker encyclopedia of the Bible*, Volume 1. Grand Rapids, MI: Baker Book House, 1988. pp. 984.

DAY 28

[1] Wiersbe, Warren W. *Be Holy: Becoming "Set Apart" For God.* OT Commentary: Leviticus. Colorado Springs, Co: David C Cook, 1994. pp. 111.

DAY 30

[1] Frost, Natasha. "For 11 Years, the Soviet Union Had No Weekends." *History.com.* https://www.history.com/news/soviet-union-stalin-weekend-labor-policy. Accessed April 2021.

DAY 31

[1] Drinkard, J. F., Jr. "Number Systems and Number Symbolism." In C. Brand, C. Draper, A. England, S. Bond, E. R. Clendenen, & T. C. Butler (Eds.), *Holman Illustrated Bible Dictionary.* Nashville, TN: Holman Bible Publishers, 2003. pp. 1200.

[2] Wiersbe, Warren W. *Be Holy: Becoming "Set Apart" For God.* OT Commentary: Leviticus. Colorado Springs, Co: David C Cook, 1994. pp. 130.

[3] ibid

DAY 32

[1] "Yom Kippur." *History.com*, October 2009. www.history.com/topics/holidays/yom-kippur-history. Accessed April 2021.

DAY 34

[1] Sklar, Jay. *Leviticus: An Introduction and Commentary.* (D. G. Firth, Ed.) (Vol. 3). Nottingham, England: Inter-Varsity Press, 2013. pp. 288-289.

DAY 35

[1] Rooker, Mark F. *Leviticus* (Vol. 3A). Nashville, TN: B&H Publishers, 2000. pp. 297.

DAY 36

[1] Swanson, J. *Dictionary of Biblical Languages with Semantic Domains : Hebrew (Old Testament)* (electronic ed.). Oak Harbor: Logos Research Systems, Inc., 1997.

[2] Sklar, Jay. *Leviticus: An Introduction and Commentary.* (D. G. Firth, Ed.) (Vol. 3). Nottingham, England: Inter-Varsity Press, 2013. pp. 302.

DAY 37

[1] Sklar, Jay. *Leviticus: An Introduction and Commentary.* (D. G. Firth, Ed.) (Vol. 3). Nottingham, England: Inter-Varsity Press, 2013. pp. 308-309.

DAY 39

[1] Rooker, Mark F. *Leviticus* (Vol. 3A). Nashville, TN: B&H Publishers, 2000. pp. 312.

DAY 40

[1] Wiersbe, Warren W. *Be Holy: Becoming "Set Apart" For God.* OT Commentary: Leviticus. Colorado Springs, Co: David C Cook, 1994. pp. 173.

RESOURCES FOR FURTHER STUDY FROM THE ESPECIALLY HARD (BUT HOLY) SECTIONS

MENSTRUATION (PAGES 90-91)

For a deeper look into a biblical view on periods, I highly recommend *A Brief Theology of Periods (Yes, Really)* by Rachel Jones.

HOMOSEXUALITY (PAGES 110-111)

If you are interested in learning more about the relationship between homosexuality and the Bible, please check out some of the following resources:

Is God Anti-Gay? by Sam Allberry
Gay Girl, Good God by Jackie Hill Perry

SLAVERY (PAGES 184-185)

If you are interested in learning more about racial reconciliation and the Church, check out:

Be the Bridge, Pursuing God's Heart for Racial Reconciliation by Latasha Morrison
ONEness EmbRACEd by Tony Evans

About Proverbs 31 Ministries

She is clothed with strength and dignity;
she can laugh at the days to come.

PROVERBS 31:25

Proverbs 31 Ministries is a nondenominational, nonprofit Christian ministry that seeks to lead women into a personal relationship with Christ. With Proverbs 31:10-31 as a guide, Proverbs 31 Ministries reaches women in the middle of their busy days through free devotions, podcast episodes, speaking events, conferences, resources, online Bible studies and training in the call to write, speak and lead others.

We are real women offering real-life solutions to those striving to maintain life's balance, in spite of today's hectic pace and cultural pull away from godly principles.

Wherever a woman may be on her spiritual journey, Proverbs 31 Ministries exists to be a trusted friend who understands the challenges she faces and walks by her side, encouraging her as she walks toward the heart of God.

Visit us online today at proverbs31.org!

Proverbs 31
MINISTRIES